Words Their Way™

Word Sorts for Derivational Relations Spellers

Second Edition

Shane Templeton
University of Nevada, Reno

Francine Johnston
University of North Carolina at Greensboro

Donald R. Bear
University of Nevada, Reno

Marcia Invernizzi
University of Virginia

Allyn & Bacon
is an imprint of

PEARSON

Boston   New York   San Francisco
Mexico City   Montreal   Toronto   London   Madrid   Munich   Paris
Hong Kong   Singapore   Tokyo   Cape Town   Sydney

Senior Editor: Linda Ashe Bishop
Senior Development Editor: Hope Madden
Senior Project Manager: Mary M. Irvin
Editorial Assistant: Demetrius Hall
Senior Art Director: Diane C. Lorenzo
Cover Designer: Ali Mohrman
Cover Image: Hope Madden
Operations Specialist: Matt Ottenweller
Director of Marketing: Quinn Perkson
Marketing Manager: Krista Clark
Marketing Coordinator: Brian Mounts

For related titles and support materials, visit our online catalog at www.pearsonhighered.com

Library of Congress Cataloging-in-Publication Data

Templeton, Shane.
   Words their way: word sorts for derivational relations spellers/Shane Templeton . . . [et al.].—2nd ed.
      p. cm.
   Rev. ed of: Words their way/by Francine Johnston, Donald Bear, Marcia Invernizzi. 1st ed. 2006.
   Includes bibliographical references.
   ISBN-13: 978-0-13-514578-4
1. English language—Orthography and spelling—Problems, exercises, etc. 2. English language—Etymology—Problems, exercises, etc. 3. English language—Roots—Problems, exercises, etc. I. Johnston, Francine R. Words their way. II. Title.
   PE1145.2.J625 2008
   428'.92—dc22

                                                                                    2008016746

Printed in the United States of America

10 9 8 7 6 5 4 3 2   [BRR]   12 11 10 09 08

Allyn & Bacon
is an imprint of

Contents

UNIT VIII   *Advanced Spelling-Meaning Patterns*   131

UNIT IX   *Prefix Assimilation*   143

Note: Every effort has been made to provide accurate and current Internet information in this book. However, the Internet and the information posted on it are constantly changing, so it is inevitable that some of the Internet addresses listed in this textbook will change.

Overview

Words Their Way: Word Sorts for Derivational Relations Spellers is intended to complement the text *Words Their Way: Word Study for Phonics, Vocabulary, and Spelling Instruction.* That core text provides a practical, research-based, and classroom-proven way to study words with students. This companion text expands and enriches that word study, specifically for derivational relations spellers. These students are typically advanced readers and writers in upper elementary, middle school, and high school.

Word study for advanced readers and writers focuses on the way spelling and vocabulary knowledge at this stage grow primarily through processes of derivation—from a single base word or word root, a number of related words are derived through the addition of prefixes and suffixes. Advanced readers, for example, are able to explore Latin and Greek word elements that are the important morphemes out of which thousands of words are constructed. This leads naturally to an exploration of spelling-meaning relationships.

Words Their Way: Word Sorts for Derivational Relations Spellers provides teachers with prepared reproducible sorts and step-by-step directions to guide students through the sorting lessons. There are follow-up activities to extend the lesson through weekly routines. The materials provided in this text will complement the use of any existing spelling and reading curricula.

SCOPE AND SEQUENCE OF THIS BOOK

Word study at the derivational relations stage focuses primarily on the structure or morphology of written words. Students systematically examine how the spelling of words visually represents meaning units, or **morphemes.** Students at this level are fairly competent spellers, so the errors they make are "higher level," requiring a more advanced foundation of spelling and vocabulary knowledge. Because of this more advanced level of word knowledge, word study at the derivational relations stage focuses as much on *vocabulary* development as it does on *spelling* development. Analyzing the spelling of words supports vocabulary growth, and vocabulary growth in turn provides helpful support for higher-level spelling development.

Vocabulary grows and develops in many ways. It is well established that certain words need to be taught systematically and deeply; that students need to do a lot of reading in order to experience and acquire over time the broad sweep of English vocabulary; and that students need to learn the processes whereby meaningful word elements or morphemes—prefixes, suffixes, base words, and word roots—combine. Linguists refer to the last type of knowledge as **generative.** Once students understand the basics according to which these important word parts combine, they can apply this knowledge to determining or *generating* the spelling and meaning of literally thousands of words. Linguists estimate that 60% to 80% of English vocabulary is created through these processes of word combinations; therefore, students who understand these processes will be well equipped to analyze and learn unfamiliar words they will encounter in their reading and their study in specific content areas.

Because this supplement focuses on generative word knowledge in spelling and vocabulary, most of the word sorts include both familiar and unfamiliar words. Knowledge of the meaning of the known words or of the meaningful word parts in the known words will enable students in most instances to infer the meanings of the unfamiliar words.

This supplement includes 60 sorts partitioned into nine units. In general, the sorts are sequenced according to morphological complexity. Early on, students examine spelling-meaning patterns as these occur primarily in known words before moving to the examination of Greek and Latin affixes and roots in later sorts. In the first three units, students will study basic processes of affixation—adding prefixes and suffixes—in words that are appropriate for examination at this level. Subsequent sorts interweave spelling-meaning patterns as they occur in words with Greek and Latin word roots and affixes.

Most sorts in this collection present 21 to 24 words each week. The words have been selected and organized based on patterns of orthographic and morphological, or spelling-meaning, relationships. In each sort, most of the words have been chosen based on their frequency in reading materials for the intermediate grades and above as well as the spelling and morphological features they represent. Expect students to spell the words in the sort and understand the spelling principles that the sorts reveal, but many of these words will not be difficult for "good" spellers in the derivational relations stage. Instead, it is word meanings and the meaning relationships that are often the objectives. In addition to—or often in place of—assessing spelling, you may wish to assess students' knowledge of the meaning of the words and word parts that have been explored in the sorts. If students are properly placed in the word study curriculum, they should already know the meaning of many of the words, be able to spell many of them, and not have to learn 21 to 24 completely new words in each lesson.

RESOURCES

Each section begins with *Notes for the Teacher* and suggestions you can use to introduce and practice the sorts. Importantly, the *Notes for the Teacher* segment often provides background information about word histories or **etymology** that should be of interest to you and your students. Sorts are presented as black line masters that can be reproduced for every student to cut apart and use for sorting.

Sorting is an essential instructional routine because it enables students to manipulate words as they look for patterns and relationships. Students should sort their own words several times over several days. We have often heard middle school and high school teachers express doubts about cutting out and sorting words. After they try it, however, they usually find that even older students enjoy the physical sorting process. It is certainly possible to write the sorts as a preparation for discussion; but writing is time consuming, and it is not easy to move words to new categories as discoveries are made.

Use the black line masters to prepare a set of words for modeling. You may want to make a transparency of the sort (reduce the size of the black line master for a better fit) and cut it apart for use on an overhead, or enlarge the words for use in a pocket chart. You can also simply make your own copy to cut apart and use on a desktop or projector. See *Words Their Way*, 4th Edition (*WTW*), and the *Words Their Way* CD-ROM (*WTWCD*) for additional background information, organizational tips, games, and activities.

PLACEMENT AND PACING

This collection of word sorts is for students who are in the derivational relations stage of spelling development. These students should already have a firm understanding of features studied in the syllable and affixes stage, including common syllable juncture patterns, spelling patterns within stressed and unstressed syllables in two-syllable words, and the effects of common prefixes and suffixes on the base words to which they are affixed. Students in the derivational relation stage might be in the upper elementary grades, but they fall primarily at the middle school level and up. To determine exactly where individual students should start, administer the upper level spelling inventory described in Chapter 2 of *Words Their Way*. This will help you determine more precisely where students at these levels should begin with their word study.

Each unit in this supplement ends with an assessment that can be used as a pretest and posttest and can also help you make decisions about where to start students in the sequence. A score of 50% to 75% usually indicates that students are ready to study the words in that unit: It is at their instructional level. A score of 90% or better indicates that students have sufficient mastery of the words and can go on to other later units. Students who score less than 50% may need to study easier features such as those presented in *Word Sorts for Syllable and Affixes Spellers*.

The pacing for these sorts is designed for average growth. After introducing a sort, you should spend about a week working with the words, though quite often you may feel that a sort may lead to 2 weeks of exploration. This may be especially true of the root sorts. Although these sorts are arranged in a sequence that builds on earlier understandings, in some cases you may decide to use the sorts out of order. Some of the Greek and Latin word root sorts, for example, can be used earlier than what we present here. In general, this collection of sorts might be considered the spelling/vocabulary curriculum for about a 2-year period, with time for extra sorts, when needed, or for review periods. Student progress through these sorts should be carefully monitored with the goal of building a good foundation for future spelling and vocabulary growth.

Placement of students in the derivational relations stage is not simply a matter of the difficulty of the spelling features as it is in earlier stages. Instead it is dependent upon the difficulty of the word meanings. For example, students in the upper elementary grades would be ready for the study of a root like *spec* in words such as *inspect* and *spectator*, but would find words like *circumspect* and *retrospective* difficult to understand and unlikely to show up in their grade-level reading materials. At the same time, those words would be very useful words for high school students to examine and learn. For this reason you will find that there are lists of additional words for most sorts. You can delete or substitute words in the existing sort and you can create your own sorts by using the template provided in the Appendix. Teachers in middle school or high school might revisit most of the units in this supplement at a higher level by using the additional word lists.

ENGLISH LANGUAGE LEARNERS

Students who would be considered in the derivational relations stage have a great deal of word knowledge, but in the case of English Language Learners (ELLs) that knowledge may be in another language. They may be ready to transfer this knowledge to English if they know enough English to make connections but may also be overwhelmed by the amount of new vocabulary these sorts may involve. ELLs will not have as many known words to use by analogy to determine the meanings of affixes and roots, so teachers may need to provide more explicit explanations instead of expecting students to make discoveries on their own. You can also reduce the number of words if desired.

Languages, such as those from Asia, may not have morphemes (roots and affixes) that combine in different ways, so the generative nature of English may be a new idea to Asian students even with advanced literacy skills in their home language. At the same time, students whose language is derived from Greek and Latin, such as Spanish and French, will find many similarities with English in the form of cognates. These cognates are common in the higher level academic vocabulary studied in the derivational relations stage; for example, *turbulence* is spelled the same in English and French (but pronounced differently) and the Spanish form is *turbulencia*. Sometimes ELLs may even have an advantage in learning academic vocabulary when cognates are used as a bridge between languages. *Tranquil* is a rare word in English whereas *tranquilo* is commonly used in Spanish. Attention to these cognates will help ELLs learn English more readily and will help native English speakers better understand the common origins of languages. Cognates can be found in resources such as *NTC's Dictionary of Spanish Cognates Thematically Organized* by R. Nash, as well as by looking through *English-Spanish* or other dictionaries in book form or online.

INTRODUCING SORTS

Sorts can be introduced in a number of ways, and the way you choose will depend on your own teaching style as well as the experience of your students. In *WTW* we describe *teacher-directed sorts, student-centered sorts*, and *Guess My Category* sorts. Most of the sorts in this book are set up for teacher-directed sorts with the categories already established with headers and key words. These sorts work well when you are introducing a new unit or if you feel that your students need more explicit modeling and explanation. However, if you wish to make word sorting into more of a constructive process where students discover the categories, you can cut off the headers before distributing the word sheets and use student-centered sorts as a way to begin. *Guess My Category* sorts also engage the students in more active thinking. Cut off the headers, but use the key words to establish the categories without giving away the feature characteristics of each category. (See *WTW* for more details on different sorting activities.)

Some words in the sorts may be unfamiliar to the students. When two related words are both unfamiliar, or for any word that is unfamiliar to the students, you have several options for introducing them.

First, wait until after sorting to explore word meanings because the sort itself (especially with words that share common roots) will help students develop hypotheses about meanings that may then be checked in a dictionary. Of course, sometimes you may simply tell students the definition in everyday terms, using the word in the context of an appropriate sentence and discussing it with students.

Second, you may scaffold or support the students' attempts to determine the meaning in the following format: Construct a one-, two-, or three-sentence context in which the target word occurs, together with two or three scaffolding questions that lead students toward an understanding of the word's meaning. For example, in Sort 16 the word pair *allude/allusion* is presented. Students may not know either word, so the base word *allude* (meaning to make an indirect reference to something) will be presented as follows:

> Brent wanted Allison to know that he realized he had acted immaturely when they went to the movie together. He didn't want to refer directly to his flipping popcorn at the screen, so instead he planned to **allude** to it by saying something like, "There probably are better ways to impress a date!"

- Did Brent want to mention the fact that he was flipping popcorn at the screen?
- How did he decide he would let Allison know he wasn't going to behave like that again?
- So, what do you think **allude** means?

A student can check the hypothesized meaning in the dictionary. Because of the suffixation pattern the students are studying, they should be able to infer the meaning of the related word in the sort, *allusion*, from an understanding of the meaning of *allude*.

As students become familiar with this format, they can take turns each week in looking ahead to the following sort you plan to use, checking the dictionary for definitions of words that are unfamiliar, and constructing their own scaffolding formats. They can then walk their fellow students through their formats.

When you introduce the sorts that include prefixes, suffixes, and base words or word roots/combining forms, you will find the teacher explanations in the *Words Their Way* chapter, "Word Study for Advanced Readers and Writers: The Derivational Relations Stage," to be helpful guides. These scripts provide examples of how to "walk through" the process in which words are formed through this combination of elements.

Many of the sorts in this text provide you with information about the etymological derivations of words in the sort. Also information is often provided about the processes of language change that have influenced spelling, pronunciation, and the meaning of words (e.g., why the spelling of some Latin roots changes across related words, as in *scribe* and *script*). Use this information at your discretion to elaborate students' understanding and to provide interesting tidbits to whet their linguistic appetites.

Below are listed standard weekly routines that involve students in repeated practice and extensions. Most can be completed by students working independently or with a partner. *Words Their Way* offers additional ideas and background information for teachers working with students in the derivational relations stage. Because scheduling for word study in middle school or high school classrooms can be a challenge, you may find this helpful.

STANDARD WEEKLY ROUTINES

1. *Repeated Work with the Words.*   Students should have their own copy of words to cut apart for sorting. We suggest that you enlarge the black line masters so that no border is left around the words on the sheets that the students receive. This will reduce the amount of waste paper and cutting time. After you have modeled and discussed the sort, students should repeat the sort several times independently. The word cards can be clipped together, or can be stored in an envelope or plastic bag to be sorted again on other days and taken home to sort for homework.

2. *Explore Word Meanings with Dictionaries.*   Copies of unabridged dictionaries with etymological information should be available in the classroom so that students can explore information about the meaning and origins of words. In addition to these classroom copies, many online dictionaries include this information as well. One source is *The American Heritage Dictionary* at http://www.yourdictionary.com. Another online source is www.onelook.com, which offers several dictionaries from which you may choose as well as an online etymological dictionary. Examples of dictionary use will be suggested throughout this supplement. Unless otherwise noted, definitions used in this supplement are from the *American Heritage Dictionary*, 4th Edition. We suggest that students keep dictionaries handy to look up words during the discussion part of lessons. Teachers can use these discussions to teach students features of dictionaries such as pronunciation guides, etymological information, multiple definitions, and so on. We do not recommend assigning students to look up and write out the definitions of more than a selected group of words, as this is not likely to stimulate interest in dictionary use; however, students can be assigned to look up at least one word and report on it to the class.

3. *Writing Sorts and Word Study/Vocabulary Notebooks.*   Students should record their word sorts by writing them into columns under the same key words that headed the columns of their word sort. Sometimes students might be asked to underline base words or indicate the accented syllables. At the bottom of the writing sort, have your students **reflect** on what they learned in that particular sort; this is especially important because many of the sorts involve learning rules about the addition of affixes to base words or word roots or learning the meanings of roots and affixes. When there are rules that may be generated, ask them to write these rules in their own words. Students might be asked to use some (not all) words in **sentences** or to **illustrate** them as a way to demonstrate their understanding of the word's meaning(s). Additional

activities for word study notebooks are included with particular sorts. A form in the Appendix can be used to structure and monitor independent work.

Students may also record new, interesting words they encounter in reading in these notebooks. A separate section, denoted by a tab, may be used to contain these words. (See the procedure for recording new words in *Words Their Way*.)

4. *Word Hunts.*   Students should look for words that mirror the features studied in the weekly word sorts in their daily reading as well as in other resources. Some features may be rare in daily reading materials so you may want to make word hunts an on-going activity where students add to previous sorts as well as the sort of the week. Students can learn to use dictionaries and online resources to find additional words. Prefixes are particularly easy to find with a dictionary, but students can learn to search by word parts that occur in the middle or at the end of words by going to online resources such as www.yourdictionary.com or www.onelook.com. At these sites you can type in an asterisk and then a word part to get a list of words (e.g., *cian for a suffix ending or *bio* for a root).

Students can also brainstorm together to think of other words that contain the same affixes, bases, or roots. After they find examples they can add the words to the bottom of the proper column in their vocabulary notebooks. You may want to create posters or displays of all the words students discover for each category. Sometimes such group efforts help students make generalizations about the frequency and usefulness of certain rules or features.

5. *Partner Work: Timed Sorts, Blind Sorts, and Writing Sorts.*   Students work to improve their automaticity in **speed sorts** and they can be motivating for students in the upper grades. After sorting the words several times, students can take turns timing each other. A **blind sort** can be used when words share different spelling patterns but similar sounds (such as *visible* and *avoidable*). Blind sorts are less useful when words are sorted simply by prefixes or roots, because the categories are usually obvious. To do a blind sort, headers or key words are laid down and students work together. One student calls out a word without showing it. The other student points to where the word should go and the partner then shows the word card to check its spelling against the key word. In a **writing sort,** the student writes the word called by a partner into the proper category, using the key word as a model for spelling. After the word has been written, the partner shows the word card to the student doing the writing to check for correctness. These sorts require students to think about words by sound and by pattern and to use the key words as models for analogy. Partner work is a great way to practice for spelling tests.

6. *Games and Other Activities.*   Create games and activities such as those in *WTW* or download them ready-made from the *WTWCD* to engage students in further practice and review. Some specific games for the derivational relations stage such as Latin Root Jeopardy, Brainburst, Assimile, and Rolling Prefixes are described in *WTW*.

7. *Assessment.*   Students can be assessed each week by asking them to spell the words they have worked with over the week. You could call out only 10 or 15 of the 24 words as a spell check. As you move farther along through the sorts, a larger proportion of the words in a particular sort may be unfamiliar to most students. Unfamiliar words, however, are usually structurally related to known words in the sort, thereby enabling students to infer their probable meanings. As an assessment activity, you can give students a few of these words and ask them to describe an activity, situation, or state of mind in which they use each word. Prepared assessments will occur at intervals throughout the supplement to test retention of particular words they have studied in each unit.

Unit 1   Prefixes

NOTES FOR THE TEACHER

Background and Objectives

In these four sorts most of the prefixes introduced in late syllables and affixes (*in-*, *un-*, *dis-*, *mis-*, *re-*, *ex-*, *pre-*) are reviewed with different words and students are introduced to eight additional prefixes (*de-*, *fore-*, *post-*, *after-*, *sub-*, *com*, *en-*, and *pro-*). Less common prefixes and assimilated prefixes are covered in later sorts. The spelling of most of these words may not be particularly challenging, as they are made up of base words that are familiar and prefixes that are spelled regularly; however, working with the sorts helps students think through the generative process of how word elements—prefixes and bases—are put together. Students will:

- Identify the prefixes and what each means
- Explain how the addition of a prefix changes the meaning of the word
- Spell these words correctly

Targeted Learners

These sorts are for students in the early derivational relations stage who will already know the spelling and meaning of most of these words but who may never have exa-mined words in categories to see the meaning connections between them. The words chosen for these sorts are suitable for students in upper elementary. For students in mid-dle and high school, you may want to prepare additional sorts or substitute more chal-lenging words from the word lists provided here. These sorts will prepare students for the longer words to come in later sorts where their ability to recognize morphemic chunks will make it easier to read and understand multisyllabic words.

Teaching Tips

Create a chart that you add to as new prefixes are introduced throughout this unit as well as throughout other units in this book. It will serve as a ready reference when students encounter words in sorts as well as in their reading materials. Students can create their own chart as part of their word study notebook.

   Word hunts will be especially fruitful when students look for words that contain the prefixes shown in these sorts. Content area textbooks or informational text may be richer in these words than fiction so include those in word hunts. The dictionary is an easy place to hunt for words with prefixes, but wherever students look, they need to consider the meanings of words when deciding if it has a prefix with a particular meaning. For example, they should avoid selecting words such as *reason, mission,* or *precious* which begin with *re-*, *mis,-* and *pre-* but do not suggest "again," "not," or "before." Students are likely to find many words that consist of a familiar prefix and attached to a root word that does not stand by itself, such as *rebellion*. Without the prefix we are left with the root *bellion*, which does not have a familiar meaning. These roots will be examined in later sorts, and you may decide to explain the difference between base words and word roots to the students. Students can look up any words that they don't know the meaning of or that they have questions about. For example, the word *rebellion* contains the prefix *re-* and the word root *-bel-*, which comes from a Latin word that means "war." *Rebellion* (and *rebel*) literally mean "to war against." This mentioning of word roots and how they function within words will plant the seed for more extensive exploration of these important elements later on. (For example, in Sort 36 the words *antebellum* and *postbellum* are examined.)

There are many additional words listed for each of these sorts. Teachers may want to create additional sorts to spend more time with these prefixes or revisit these prefixes with harder words after students have studied the spelling features and Greek and Latin roots that make them more challenging. For example, *dejection* will be better understood after the study of words that end in *-tion* and the study of the Latin root *-ject-* meaning "throw."

Games from *WTW* that can be adapted for the features explored in this unit include Jeopardy, Card Categories, I'm Out, Word Study Pursuit, Word Study Uno, and other games described in Chapter 6. The card game Quartet described in Chapter 8 of *WTW* can also be adapted to review prefixes.

Many of the prefixes that are covered in this unit occur in Spanish and are easily recognized in some cognates: *intolerente* (*intolerant*), *explorar* (*explore*), *inflar* (*inflate*), *revisar* (*revise*), *preparar* (*prepare*), *submarino* (*submarine*), *compuesto* (*compound*), *proveer* (*provide*), and *encontrar* (*encounter*). The negative or opposite sense of *un-*, *dis-*, *mis-*, and *de-* do not exist in Spanish but are substituted with the prefix *des-* as in *desconocido* (*unknown*), *deshonra* (*dishonest*), *descorazonar* (*discourage*), and *desinflar* (*deflate*). *Ante-* and *pre-* are used instead of *fore-* (*foreboding* = *presentimiento*), and *pos-* is used instead of *post-* and *after-* (*posponer* for *postpone*). A Spanish/English dictionary will help you find more examples of these.

SORT 1   PREFIXES (*IN-*, *UN-*, *DIS-*, *MIS-*)

Demonstrate, Sort, and Reflect

(See page 13.) All of these prefixes change the base word to a negative meaning or to an opposite meaning. Prepare a set of words to use for teacher-directed modeling. Save the discussion of word meanings until after sorting. Display a transparency of the words on the overhead or hand out the sheet of words to the students. Ask them what they notice about the words and get ideas about how the words can be sorted. Students usually notice that all the words contain prefixes. Remind them of the terms **prefixes** (units added to the beginning of a word) and **base word** (the word to which prefixes and suffixes are added). Put up the headers (*un-*, *in-*, *dis-*, *mis-*) and the bolded key words and then sort the rest of the words.

The discussion after the first sort might go something like this: "Look at the words under *un-*. What do you notice about the meanings of these words?" Focus on the key word *uneasy*. Ask students for the base word. Explain that a prefix has been added to the base word and that it changes the meaning of the word. Ask students what *uneasy* means (a feeling that is the opposite of easy or not easy). Repeat this with the other words under *un-*, talking about the meaning of each word. Then remind students that a prefix has a meaning of its own and ask them what *un-* means in the first list of words (it means "not" or "the opposite of"). Repeat this with the words under *in-* ("not"), *mis-* ("bad" or "badly"), and *dis-* ("not" or "the opposite of") to review the meaning of each prefix. Students can write these meanings on their headers. Some words will not be literal reversals of the base word. Ask students if they've thought about how *disease* can literally mean "the opposite of" *ease*? *Mistake* and *mischief* clearly have negative meanings but are not really the opposite of the base words *take* and *chief*. Point out the double *s* in the commonly misspelled word *misspell* and ask students why there must be two. (One goes with the prefix and one with the base word.)

in-	*un-*	*dis-*	*mis-*
insincere	**uneasy**	**dishonest**	**misspell**
informal	unaware	disbelief	misfortune
infrequent	unknown	disorder	mistake
inhuman	undress	disconnect	misleading
inexpensive	unfasten	disease	mischief
insane	untidy	disrespect	
		discourage	

Extend

Students should go on *word hunts* in familiar reading material to locate as many words as they can with these same prefixes. They may find words like *inside* and *inject* where the prefix *in-* suggests "into" rather than "not." Just have them add these in another column for now (they will study them in the next sort). There will also be some "exceptions"; that is, words such as *uncle* and *reach* that do not have identifiable prefixes because there is no base word or root left when the prefix is removed. These are known as *false prefixes*.

Additional Words.

un- *unattached, unbroken, unarmed, unaided, unbearable, uncomfortable, uncommon, unconscious, unexpected, unfortunate, unfriendly, unglued, ungrateful, unheated, unlucky, unpopular, unravel, unreasonable, unsuccessful, untangle, untouched, unplanned, unworthy*

in- *inability, inaccurate, inadequate, inaudible, incapable, inconsiderate, inconvenient, incredible, incurable, indigestion, indirect, inefficient, inexperienced, inflexible*

dis- *disadvantage, disappoint, disapprove, disarm, disaster, discard, discontinue, discord, discount, discharge, disfigure, disgrace, distrust, disinfect, disjointed, dislocated, dismount, disown, disprove, disqualify, distaste, distract, distress*

mis- *misbehave, misconduct, misfit, misgivings, misprint, misstep, mistrusted, misused, misunderstood*

SORT 2 PREFIXES (*PRE-, FORE-, POST-, AFTER-*)

Demonstrate, Sort, and Reflect

(See page 14.) You can introduce this sort in a manner similar to Sort 1, but students can probably sort by prefixes without much introduction. *Pre-* and *fore-* both mean "before" whereas *post-* and *after-* both mean "after." Spend time discussing with students the meanings of the prefixes and words. The word *prefix* offers an excellent opportunity for thinking explicitly about what this term means: literally, "to fix before." The *pre-* in *preposition* is pronounced differently (as it is in *preface*) but talk about the base word and how a preposition is a part of speech that comes before a position as in "up the hill" or "under the covers." Compare and contrast *preseason/postseason, forethought/afterthought,* and *foreword/afterword.* The latter word pair may be illustrated by showing the students a book that has a foreword and an afterword. A foreword is usually written by someone other than the author. If the word *preface* does not come up in this discussion, you may choose to mention it: It literally means "to speak before" and, in contrast to a foreword, is usually written by the author.

pre-	fore-	post-	after-
prepare	**foretell**	**postpone**	**afternoon**
predict	foreman	postwar	afterword
preface	foreword	postseason	afterthought
prehistoric	forefathers	postdate	aftertaste
precede	foresight	posttest	
prefix	forethought		
preseason			
preposition			
prewar			

Additional Words.

pre- *precedent, predate, predetermine, preexisting, prejudice, preliminary, premier, premium, premonition, preoccupied, preventative, previous*

fore- *forecourt, forefinger, foregone, foreground, forehand, foreknowledge, foreordained, forepaw, forerunner, foreshadow, forewarning*

post- *posthumous, postscript, postcolonial, postdated, postmortem, posterior, postmodern, postgraduate*

after- *afterlife, aftermath, aftereffects, afterglow, aftershocks, afterworld*

SORT 3   PREFIXES (*RE-, EX-, IN-, DE-*)

Demonstrate, Sort, and Reflect

(See page 15.) Introduce this sort in a manner similar to Sort 1 but be aware that many of these words do not have a base that stands alone. Begin the discussion with words that have a base word that is clearly affected by the prefix and can be interpreted literally. *Replay* means to "play again" or "play back." Some words cannot be interpreted so literally but should be words that are familiar to the students. For example, they should be able to see how *inflate* and *interior* are related to "into" even though the base words are unclear in meaning. *Re-* can mean either "again" or "back," *ex-* means "out of" or "beyond," *de-* means "to take away," and *in-* is revisited here in words where it means "into" or "inside" as in *inflate.*

re-	in-	ex-	de-
replay	**inflate**	**exhale**	**deflate**
reappear	interior	exile	defrost
reclaim	inhabit	explore	deprive
reconsider	inmate	excess	decrease
reruns	install	exhaust	delete
research	inhale	exterior	
reaction			

Extend

Look for antonyms (*inhale, exhale, interior, exterior, deflate, inflate*) and challenge students to use them in sentences: *The exterior of the little house was shabby but the interior was clean and tidy.*

Take all the *in-* words from last week and this week and mix them up. Then ask students to sort them by whether the meaning refers to "not" or "in."

Create the card game Quartet described in Chapter 8 of *WTW* using the eight prefixes covered so far. Require students to add the meaning when they ask for matches: "Give me any cards you have with the prefix *in-* meaning 'not'."

De- occurs in many words (*dessert, decade, delicate*) that do not suggest "away from," so in word hunts students need to consider the meaning of the word carefully.

Additional Words.

re- rearrange, reassure, recline, recover, reforest, refrain, reimburse, revolt, revolution, repair, repellent, replacement, respond, restrain, revenge, reverse, retrieve, retreat

ex- excavate, excellent, excerpt, except, exception, exchange, excrete, excursion, exempt, exhibit, exodus, exoskeleton, exotic, explode, export, exposure, extent, extinct, extract, extremity

in- (in, inside) inborn, incite, incision, include, infection, inference, influence, ingredient, injection, inquire, inscription, insight, insert, install, intrude, invasion, investment

de- debug, decaffeinated, decanter, decapitate, decongestant, decontaminate, deficient, deforestation, defuse, degenerate, degrading, dehydrated, demerit, demolish, demoralized, denominator, denounce, deodorant, deplete, deported, deposed, depreciate, deprived, derived, desegregate, detached, detract, deviate

SORT 4   PREFIXES (*SUB-*, *COM-*, *PRO-*, *EN-*)

(See page 16.) In this group of prefixes the meaning of *sub-* and *com-* are straightforward, *sub-* meaning "below" or "under" as in *subway* and *com-* meaning "with" or "together" as in *combine*. In these words *en-* occurs in verbs and generally suggests "causing something to happen" as in *encourage*. Compare *encourage* with *discourage* from an earlier sort. *Pro-* is a common prefix but is harder to pin down in terms of its meaning. In these words it suggests "for," "forward," or "in favor of" as in *promote* (literally, "to move forward"). Word hunts will turn up many words beginning with *pro-* whose meaning will not be clearly related to this.

sub-	com-	pro-	en-
subway	**combine**	**propel**	**enable**
subset	company	propose	encourage
submarine	companion	protect	entrust
subtotal	compound	provider	endanger
subtitle	compress	promote	enforce
submerge	comrade	progress	enlarge

Additional Words.

sub- subatomic, subcommittee, subconscious, subcontinent, subculture, subliminal, subplot, subservient, subsidiary, subsidize, substandard, subtraction, subtrahend, subterranean, suburban, subversive

com- committee, commune, communicate, communism, community, compact, compassion, compatible, competition, compile, complement, component, composite, comprise

pro- *proceed, procure, profess, prologue, propagate, procreate, propaganda, proponent, proscribe, proselytize, prospector, protracted, provoke, provisions*
en- *enclose, endorse, endow, engrave, engrossed, enhance, enjoy, enlighten, enlist, enrage, enroll, entangle, entice, entitle, envelop*

ASSESSMENT 1 FOR SORTS 1–4

(See page 17.) Ask students to match each prefix with its meaning. Below is the answer key.

1. *mis-* (d)	a. not	1. *dis-* (b)	a. out of
2. *pre-* (c)	b. cause	2. *fore-* (e)	b. not
3. *re-* (f)	c. before	3. *ex-* (a)	c. take away
4. *in-* (a)	d. badly	4. *in-* (g)	d. under
5. *post-* (e)	e. after	5. *sub-* (d)	e. before
6. *com-* (g)	f. again or back	6. *de-* (c)	f. for
7. *en-* (b)	g. with	7. *pro-* (f)	g. into

Ask students to spell and define the following words. It is fine to use the word as part of the definition as in *endanger—to put someone in danger.*

1. misfortune	**2.** untidy	**3.** discourage
4. insane	**5.** predict	**6.** reconsider
7. foretell	**8.** misspell	**9.** defrost
10. endanger	**11.** protect	**12.** subtitle
13. comrade	**14.** exterior	**15.** postpone

SORT 1   Prefixes (*in-*, *un-*, *dis-*, *mis-*)

in-	*un-*	*dis-*	*mis-*
uneasy		**insincere**	**dishonest**
misspell		unaware	informal
disbelief		misfortune	unknown
infrequent		disorder	mistake
undress		inhuman	disconnect
misleading		unfasten	inexpensive
disease		mischief	untidy
insane		disrespect	discourage

SORT 2   Prefixes (*pre-*, *fore-*, *post-*, *after-*)

pre-	*fore-*	*post-*	*after-*
prepare	**foretell**		**postpone**
afternoon	predict		foreman
postwar	prefix		preface
foreword	postseason		afterthought
prehistoric	forefathers		postdate
aftertaste	precede		foresight
posttest	preseason		preposition
forethought	afterword		prewar

SORT 3   Prefixes (*re-*, *ex-*, *in-*, *de-*)

re-	ex-	in-	de-
replay		**inflate**	**exhale**
deflate	reappear		interior
exile	defrost		reclaim
inhabit	explore		deprive
reconsider	inmate		excess
decrease	reruns		exhaust
delete	research		inhale
exterior	reaction		install

SORT 4   Prefixes (*sub-, com-, pro-, en-*)

sub-	*com-*	*pro-*	*en-*
subway	**combine**		**propel**
enable	subset		company
promote	encourage		submarine
companion	propose		entrust
subtotal	compound		protect
endanger	subtitle		compress
provider	enforce		submerge
comrade	progress		enlarge

Assessment 1 for Sorts 1–4
Beside each prefix write the letter of the matching meaning.

Name _____

1. dis-	a. out of
2. fore-	b. not
3. ex-	c. take away
4. in-	d. under
5. sub-	e. before
6. de-	f. for
7. pro-	g. into

1. mis-	a. not
2. pre-	b. cause
3. re-	c. before
4. in-	d. badly
5. post-	e. after
6. com-	f. again/back
7. en-	g. with

Unit II   Derivational Suffixes

NOTES FOR THE TEACHER

Background and Objectives

When derivational suffixes are added to base words several things happen. First the grammatical function of the word usually changes. The verb *deliver* becomes the noun *delivery*, the adjective *straight* becomes the verb *straighten*. Sometimes there is a spelling change as when the final *e* in *pure* is dropped in *purify* and the *y* in *colony* changes to an *i* in *colonize*. Accent or stress often changes also. The first syllable of **hu**mid is accented but the accent shifts to the second syllable hu**mid**ity. Finally, the sound of some letters change or alternate. Listen to the long sound of *o* in *compose* change to the schwa sound in *composition*. The final /s/ in *race* becomes /sh/ in *racial*. All of these changes except the sound changes will be explored in these sorts. Consonant and vowel alternation will be explored in later units.

Suffixes are taught in these nine sorts beginning with a review of some introduced in the late syllables and affixes (*-er, -est, -y, -ly, -ful, -ness,* and *-less*). Since suffixes change the grammatical function there will be much attention to parts of speech in theses sorts. Although many of these suffixes will be familiar to students, some of the words in which these affixes occur are more appropriate for study in higher grades. For example, words such as *murkier/murkiest* and *stodgier/stodgiest* are less familiar or unknown. Other words lend themselves to exploration of more abstract or *metaphorical* meaning as, for example, *fruitless*, which can literally mean "without fruit," but has acquired a more metaphorical meaning. Suffixes have meanings (*-ory*, for example, means "of or relating to") but the meanings are often abstract and are not explicitly taught the same way prefixes are taught. The spelling of most of these words may not be particularly challenging, as they are made up of base words that are familiar and affixes that are spelled regularly; however, working with the sorts helps students think through the generative process of how word elements—prefixes, suffixes, and bases—are put together. Students will:

- Identify the suffixes
- Explain how the addition of a suffix changes the part of speech
- Spell these words correctly

Targeted Learners

This unit of study is most appropriate for early derivational relations spellers. It continues to prepare students to examine multisyllabic words for base words and affixes. Because some of these endings have been studied in the late syllables and affixes stage you may want to skip Sorts 5, 6, and 8. However, the sorts in this book use different words that are generally at a higher level and review the rules for adding endings that involve a spelling change such as *e*-drop, doubling, or changing the *y* to *i*.

Teaching Tips

You may want to create a chart of derivational suffixes and the part of speech they signal. Add to it as different suffixes are studied. The chart can be reviewed frequently even beyond the explicit study of suffixes as students examine words throughout this book. The final chart might look something like this with the addition of suffixes from future units. Students can create a similar chart in their word study notebooks as each new suffix is added.

Nouns	Adjectives	Verbs	Adverbs
-ness laziness	-y funny, frosty	-en frighten	-ly slowly, merrily
-ary/-ery/-ory library, bravery, victory	-er faster, lazier	-ize idolize	
-ty/-ity safety, actvity	-est fastest, laziest	-ify classify	
-er/-or speaker, creator	-ful delightful	-ate decorate	
-ian guardian, musician	-less painless		
-ist artist	-ary/-ory imaginary, satisfactory		
-al/-ial arrival, memorial	-ic magnetic		
-ment payment	-al logical		
-ion action, possession*	-ous/ious dangerous, furious		
-ence/-ance confidence, brilliance*	-ent/-ant confident, brilliant*		
-ency/-ancy emergency	-able/-ible dependable, legible*		

*Introduced in later units

Games from *WTW* that can be adapted for the features explored in this unit include Jeopardy, Card Categories, I'm Out, Word Study Pursuit, Word Study Uno, and other games described in Chapter 6. The games Brainburst, Word Building, and Quartet described in Chapter 8 of *WTW* can be adapted to review suffixes.

There are Spanish counterparts to many of the suffixes studied in this unit and students who are native speakers of Spanish learning English or native English speakers learning Spanish will have a better understanding of the other language through attention to cognates. For example, the suffix *-ic* has the counterpart *-ico* in Spanish (*magnetico*). Words that end in *-ty* and *-ity* in English often end in *-dad* in Spanish (*authority = autoridad, formality = formalidad*). The meaning of suffixes such as *-ful* and *-ness* are represented in a variety of ways: *respectful = respetuoso, thankful = agradecido,* and *happiness = felicidad*.

Comparatives (*-er, -est*) are not handled with affixes in Spanish and many other languages but are widely used in English and need to be understood by ELLs.

SORT 5   SUFFIXES (*-Y, -LY, -ILY*)

Demonstrate, Sort, and Reflect

(See page 31.) Prepare a set of words to use for teacher-directed modeling. Display a transparency of the words on the overhead or hand out the sheet of words to the students. Ask them what they notice about the words and get ideas about how the words can be sorted. Students usually notice that the words end in *-y, -ly,* and *-ily*. Introduce the term **suffix** if the students do not use it and contrast it with **prefix** used in earlier sorts. Put up the headers and sort the words as shown below. Then talk about the meaning of the words and what the suffix does to the base word. Help students articulate that adding a *y* to the base word creates an adjective whereas adding -*ly* and -*ily* creates an adverb. Try out the adjectives in sentences such as, "I heard a _____ sound," or "The _____ dog ran off." Try out adverbs in sentences such as, "The boy answered (or walked) _____," or "The girl read (or ate) _____."

-y	-ly	-ily
scratchy	**silently**	**merrily**
squirmy	secretly	greedily
velvety	rapidly	hastily
squeaky	fluently	readily
wealthy	eagerly	
skinny	generously	
swampy	seriously	
shaggy	politely	
silvery	briefly	
spotty	bravely	

Extend

Underline the base word in each word and help students identify those where the spelling changes: *spotty, skinny,* and *shaggy* double the final consonant before *y. Merrily, hastily, greedily,* and *readily* change the final *y* to *i* before adding -*ly*. Find base words that end in *e* and discuss why the *e* was not dropped before -*ly* (the suffix begins with a consonant, not a vowel): *bravely, falsely, politely.*

Students will find many words ending in -*y* and -*ly* on a word hunt. Help them test the words for the part of speech. *Bakery* ends in *y* but it is not an adjective. *Lovely* ends in -*ly* but is an adjective rather than an adverb.

Additional Words. *flowery, frosty, pricey, guilty, shabby, spooky, starry, sweaty, watery, healthy, powdery, unlucky, scruffy, shadowy, wooly, awkwardly, barely, firmly, loudly, warmly, weakly, wildly, audibly, bleakly, briefly, cheaply, faintly, harshly, proudly, sternly, sweetly, bitterly, cleverly, frugally, publicly, tenderly, unfairly, viciously, clumsily, drearily, dizzily, messily, steadily, uneasily*

SORT 6   COMPARATIVE SUFFIXES (-ER, -EST, -IER, -IEST)

Demonstrate, Sort, and Reflect

(See page 32.) Prepare a set of words to use for teacher-directed modeling. Display a transparency of the words on the overhead or hand out the sheet of words to the students. Ask them what they notice about the words and get ideas about how the words can be sorted. Students usually notice that all the words end in -*er* or -*est*. Sort first by -*er* and -*est* and talk about the meaning of the words and what the suffix does to the base word. (When comparing two things, -*er* is used. When comparing more than two things, use -*est*.) Create sentences that demonstrate the difference.

Then match up the pairs *kinder* and *kindest*. Talk about how the suffixes -*er* and -*est* were simply added to the base word *kind*. Then pair up *emptier* and *emptiest*. Ask for the base word and write it up: *empty*. Ask students how the spelling of the base word changed: The -*y* was changed to *i* before -*er* and -*est* were added. Ask students to underline the base words in each pair. Sort the rest of the words under the key words as shown below. Discuss the meanings of any words students might not know such as *murkier* or *crummier* and ask them to come up with ideas about murky or crummy situations: "The fog made the afternoon even *murkier* than the morning, but in the evening the darkness made it *murkiest* of all."

Sort these words into two new categories under -*ier* and -*iest*. Ask the students to form a generalization that covers these words (e.g., when a word ends in *y*, change the *y* to *i* before adding the suffix).

-er	-est	-ier	-iest
kinder	**kindest**	**earlier**	**earliest**
stranger	strangest	emptier	emptiest
cleaner	cleanest	trickier	trickiest
quieter	quietest	fancier	fanciest
harsher	harshest	crummier	crummiest
		murkier	murkiest
		shinier	shiniest

Extend

To review the rules involved in adding suffixes, sort the words as shown below.

e-drop	Change *y* to *i*	Nothing
stranger	emptier	cleaner
strangest	earlier	cleanest
	trickier	quieter
	trickiest	quietest
	fancier	harsher
	fanciest	harshest
	crummier	
	crummiest	
	murkier	
	murkiest	
	shinier	
	shiniest	

Extend

A picture book by Judi Barrett entitled, *Things That Are Most in the World*, raises questions about superlatives on each page ("What is the smelliest thing in the world") and supplies an answer ("a skunk convention"). It may inspire your students to create their own superlatives by answering questions such as, "What is the shiniest thing in the world? What is the strangest thing in the world?"

To help students **transfer** their understanding of the rules for adding these affixes, ask them to add -*er* and -*est* to these 10 words: *dense, deadly, sunny, sweet, brave, hungry, lucky, safe, smooth, moist*. A word hunt will turn up many words ending in -*er* that are not comparatives, such as *teacher* or *skater*. Require students to think carefully about the word meaning and part of speech before adding it to their word hunt lists.

Many comparatives in English (and other languages) are formed with the use of *more* and *most* rather than *-er* or *-est*. Learning when to use the prefixes and when to use the words is a challenge. We say, "I feel happier" today but "I feel more cheerful." You might ask students to look for examples of both during a word hunt.

Additional Words.   *bleaker, brighter, fresher, stronger, sweeter, wilder, chewier, dressier, groovier, happier, healthier, lovelier, messier, noisier, prettier, scratchier, scrawnier, sleazier, sneakier, thirstier, wealthier, wobblier, yummier*

SORT 7   NOUN SUFFIXES (-*ER*, -*OR*, -*IAN*, -*IST*)

(See page 33.) All of these suffixes indicate agents, someone or something that does, or is related to the base word. The suffixes *-er* and *-or* are common and are often added to a verb to create a noun that names a "doer."

Sort and Reflect

Students should be able to sort these words easily by the suffix. Read through each list of words and talk about the base word and how the suffix changes the meaning and the way the word is used in a sentence. The *-ian* suffix has several sounds and students may pronounce the words slightly different but they are all spelled the same. The *-ian* suffix is explored further in Sort 15 when its sound is clearly /shun/ as in *musician* and is compared to words ending in *-ion*.

-er	-or	-ian	-ist
speaker	**creator**	**guardian**	**artist**
traveler	visitor	Asian	finalist
prisoner	decorator	historian	terrorist
defender	director	Australian	specialist
believer	inventor	librarian	vocalist
attacker	survivor	civilian	
admirer			

Extend

Pull out the words in which the base word ends in either *-e* (*believe*) or *-y* (*history*) and review with students the spelling generalizations at work when the suffix is added. A word hunt will turn up many words that end in *-er* and *-or* but they will not all be nouns that name agents. Ask students to consider the meaning of the words as they did in the last sort where comparatives were the target feature.

The suffix *-ian* is added informally to many place names to identify people from that place: *Bostonian, Washingtonian, Virginian, Pennsylvanian, Californian.* Is this true in your town or state? If not, what term is used? (*Texan, New Yorker,* etc.)

Additional Words.   *announcer, borrower, complainer, consumer, crusader, employer, examiner, hijacker, hitchhiker, kidnapper, listener, mourner, murderer, reporter, rescuer, southerner, trespasser, writer, conductor, contractor, counselor, governor, illustrator, instructor, narrator, negotiator, operator, prospector, sculptor, spectator, successor, surveyor, warrior, disciplinarian, Egyptian, Hawaiian, pedestrian, valedictorian, biologist, bicyclist, cartoonist, colonist, columnist, druggist, ecologist, geologist, motorcyclist, naturalist, organist, receptionist, stylist, therapist, violinist*

SORT 8   SUFFIXES (-*MENT*, -*LESS*, -*NESS*)

Sort and Reflect

(See page 34.) Students should be able to do this as a student-centered sort and establish the categories for themselves. If they put all the words ending in -*lessness* with -*ness*, these can be separated out later. Discuss with students how the suffixes change the meaning and use of the word. Begin by establishing what the base word means and its part of speech; *Pay* is a verb that means "to give someone money" and *payment* is "the act of doing it" as in, *I made a car payment*. Help students conclude that the suffix -*ment* creates nouns out of verbs and suggests an action or process. The suffix -*ness* creates nouns out of adjectives and suggests a "state of being" as in *laziness*. The suffix -*less* creates adjectives that mean "without" as in *breathless*. The word *priceless* is interesting; literally, it means "without price" and students may ask whether it means something that is so worthless or cheap that it literally has no price. Theoretically it could, of course; but the meaning of the word *priceless* has evolved over the years to mean something that is so incredibly valuable that you could not put a price on it. The words ending in -*lessness* have changed from a noun to an adjective and back to a noun with the addition of suffixes. They are long words but should be easy to break into parts and spell. Separate these out even though there is no special header.

Draw students' attention to the base words and ask them to find any whose spellings have been changed before adding these suffixes. They should see that words ending in a consonant or *e* simply add the endings that start with consonants and do not require any such changes. Base words that end in *y*, however, must change the *y* to *i* (*laziness, dizziness, friendliness, saltiness, emptiness*).

-*ment*	-*less*	-*ness*	
payment	**breathless**	**laziness**	**powerlessness**
replacement	hopeless	blindness	fearlessness
employment	thoughtless	dizziness	
punishment	priceless	politeness	
agreement	flawless	friendliness	
amusement	tactless	emptiness	
government	fruitless	saltiness	

Extend

Words hunts should turn up many more words with these suffixes. Encourage students to look for the suffix inside words such as *carelessly*.

Challenge students to create more words from other words in the sort that end in -*less*: *thoughtlessness, hopelessness, tactlessness,* and so forth. Remind them of the -*ly* suffix and ask them to find words to which they can add the ending as in *breathlessly* and *thoughtlessly*. How does adding -*ly* change the way the word is used? It is now an adverb that describes how something was done.

Additional Words.   *alignment, argument, adjustment, assessment, attachment, commitment, enforcement, engagement, equipment, impeachment, improvement, nourishment, placement, readjustment, refreshment, requirement, resentment, retirement, settlement, shipment, statement, treatment, ceaseless, cloudless, colorless, fatherless, flavorless, humorless, penniless, powerless, sleeveless, speechless, weightless, awareness, attentiveness, craziness, holiness, juiciness, looseness, messiness, shortness, sweetness, tenseness, thickness, ugliness, weirdness, hopelessness, recklessness, tastelessness, pennilessness, restlessness*

SORT 9   SUFFIXES (-ARY, -ERY, -ORY)

(See page 35.) The endings *-ary*, *-ery*, and *-ory* generally signal nouns or adjectives. In these words there is not always a base word. *Bravery* is clearly a noun related to the adjective base word *brave*, but *category* does not have a base word. This sort is included here with a focus on the different spelling and sounds of this ending.

Demonstrate, Sort, and Reflect

Go over the meaning of any words that you think students might not know. Save the discussion of *stationary* and *stationery* for later. Sort first by the ending pattern (*-ary*, *-ory*, and *-ery*). *Century* will be an oddball (only a few words in English end with *-ury* or *-iry*). Read the words in each column emphasizing the final ending. The words ending in *-ary* should all sound alike. Put up the sound header for this column (/ary/). Then read all the words under *-ery*, listening for the sound. Help students find the oddball *stationery* that sounds like /ary/. Look at the words that end with *-ory* and help students identify two sounds. Put up the header *-ory* for the words with that sound. Then compare the other *-ory* words with the words under *-ery* to establish that they have the same sound, /schwa + ry/. Put these together into one column. Talk about how these will be the trickiest to spell because they sound the same at the end but are spelled two ways.

Pull out the homophones *stationary* and *stationery* and compare the spellings. The endings sound the same but are spelled differently. Talk about the meaning of the words and how to know which word to use. One mnemonic device is that both *stationery* and *lett**er*** have an *-er*.

-ary	-ery	-ory	oddball
imaginary	**bravery**	**category**	**stationery***
secretary	machinery	lavatory	century
library	mystery	inventory	
military	scenery	dormitory	
ordinary	delivery	directory	
necessary	grocery	victory	
February		history	
January			
stationary*			

*Homophones

Extend

Find words that are built with familiar base words: *bravery, machinery, scenery, delivery, imaginary*. Talk about what effect the *-ery* ending has on the word. Generally these three endings create words that are nouns, but sometimes adjectives. Challenge students to sort their words by the part of speech.

> **Nouns:** *library, stationery, territory, memory, mystery, century*, etc.
> **Adjectives:** *ordinary, necessary, stationary, imaginary*
> *Military* can be either an adjective (*military strength*) or a noun (*he joined the military*).

This feature should be reinforced with a blind sort because it requires careful listening. Students will find more words in a word hunt. Some of these may not fit the categories established here (such as the /ary/ spelled with *-ery* in *cemetery*) but students can list them as oddballs.

Additional Words.

-ary = /arÿ/ *adversary, arbitrary, contrary, culinary, customary, dictionary, extraordinary, hereditary, honorary, literary, primary, planetary, obituary, revolutionary, sanctuary, solitary, temporary, voluntary*

ary = **schwa** + **ry** *anniversary, boundary, elementary, glossary, salary, summary, infirmary*

-ory = /orÿ/ *auditory, allegory, depository, expository, laboratory, mandatory, observatory, respiratory, territory, transitory*

-ory = /schwa + rÿ/ *accessory, compulsory, satisfactory, theory, unsavory, factory*

-ery = /schwa + rÿ/ *artery, artillery, greenery, grocery, imagery, lottery, misery, nursery, robbery, savagery, shrubbery, slavery, sorcery, surgery, treachery, trickery, upholstery, winery*

-ery = /arÿ/ *cemetery, confectionery, dysentery, monastery*

SORT 10   SUFFIXES (-TY, -ITY)

(See page 36.) In this sort students will consider what effect the suffixes have upon the base words. In these words *-ty* and *-ity* change adjectives to nouns and suggest a "condition" or "quality." In addition, the accent often shifts from the first syllable (*active*) to the second (*activity*) or the syllable right before the suffix.

The suffix *-ity* or *-ty* has a number of Spanish cognates with the *-dad* ending: *avtividad, tranquilidad, humedad, novedad,* and *seguridad* (*safety*).

Demonstrate, Sort, and Reflect

You may want to do this as a teacher-directed sort. First sort the words by the suffixes *-ty* and *-ity*. Pronounce the words as you sort so that students hear the sound difference (*-ity* is distinct from *-ty*). Then match the base words to the derived words. Ask students to identify the part of speech of the base words (they are all adjectives that describe things, including *novel* which has two distinct meanings). Then talk about the meanings of each pair and how the suffix changes the adjective to a noun. *Casualty* is a curious word. Have students look up both the base word and the derived word. It means one who is injured or killed, or an accident. Hardly the meaning we associate with *casual* (relaxed or informal).

Go back through the pairs again but this time talk about the accented syllables in each to focus attention on the change (i.e., *festive, festivity*). Underline the accented syllable in each pair under *-ity* and ask students to do the same.

baseword	-ty	baseword	-ity
safe	**safety**	**active**	**activity**
special	specialty	festive	festivity
novel	novelty	tranquil	tranquility
royal	royalty	humid	humidity
casual	casualty	minor	minority
certain	certainty	sensitive	sensitivity

Extend

Pull out *safe/safety, sensitive/sensitivity, active/activity,* and *festive/festivity* and ask students how the spelling in the base word changed before adding *-ty* and *-ity* (the final *e* is dropped before *-ity* [a suffix beginning with a vowel] but not before the *-ty*). A word hunt should simply focus on finding more words that end in both *-ty* and *-ity*. They will not all have clear base words as in *dignity*. Word hunts will turn up many words that end in *-ty* where the *y* has been added to a base word ending in final *t* to create an adjective such as *rusty, thirsty, tasty*. Help students distinguish these from the nouns that end in *-ty* and *-ity*.

The game *Stressbusters* described in Chapter 7 of *WTW* might be used to focus attention on accented syllables.

Additional Words.   *hostility, humanity, passivity, popularity, priority, reality, relativity, stupidity, timidity, validity, amnesty, anxiety, certainty, difficulty, gaiety, liberty, plenty, poverty, property, puberty, subtlety, travesty, uncertainty, warranty*

SORT 11   SUFFIXES (-*AL*, -*IAL*, -*IC*)

(See page 37.) The suffixes *-al*, *-ial*, and *-ic* often signal adjectives derived from nouns (*fiction-fictional, hero-heroic*). They can also signal nouns derived from verbs (*arrive, arrival*). They all suggest "associated with" or "relating to."

The suffix *-ic* has the counterpart *-ico* in some Spanish cognates (*magnético, alphabético, poético, héroico*).

Sort and Reflect

Students can probably sort these words into categories independently using the headers provided on the sort. After sorting, talk about the meaning of the words in each category as well as their part of speech. Help students see that anything that is *fictional* is related to *fiction* or describes something that is not true as in a "fictional land" such as Narnia (C.S. Lewis) or Middle Earth (J.R.R. Tolkien). Some of the words are nouns but still suggest "relating to" as in when we *bury* someone it is a *burial*. Test adjectives in a sentence like, "The news was _____." Test nouns in a sentence such as, "We talked about the _____ we saw yesterday."

-al	-ial	-ic
fictional	**burial**	**magnetic**
comical	territorial	poetic
accidental	industrial	Islamic
arrival	tutorial	alphabetic
logical	memorial	heroic
betrayal	editorial	patriotic
musical		rhythmic
global		angelic
coastal		dramatic

Extend

Identify the base words by underlining them after writing them in a word study notebook activity. Identify those whose spelling changes (*e*-drop or change *y* to *i*). Accent sometimes changes (*accident, accidental*) and sometimes does not (*fiction-fictional*). Help students sort words by those in which the accent changes (*territorial, industrial, memorial*, etc.) and those in which the accent does not change (*critical, arrival, betrayal*, etc.).

Sort words by part of speech (nouns, verbs, and adjectives). Some words like *tutorial* can be both a noun and an adjective.

A word hunt should simply focus on finding more words that end with these suffixes (they will not all have clear base words as in *chemical* or *crucial*). Students should find that most words ending in *-al* are adjectives but some are not (*cathedral, rehearsal*).

Help students identify the parts of speech. Some words can act as adjectives or nouns such as *official*.

Additional Words.   *alphabetical, analytical, bridal, classical, clinical, critical, herbal, marginal, personal, rental, rehearsal, removal, reversal, revival, bacterial, material, ceremonial, alcoholic, apologetic, Arabic, atomic, diplomatic, Germanic, graphic, organic, realistic, satanic, symbolic, Icelandic*

SORT 12   ADJECTIVE SUFFIXES (-*FUL*, -*OUS*, -*IOUS*)

(See page 38.) These three derivational suffixes suggest "full of" or "having the qualities of." They have been added to base words that are mostly nouns to create adjectives. *Outrageous* is an oddball because it ends with -*eous*, retaining the *e* to keep the *g* soft. Identify words whose spelling changes (*envy, study, glory,* and *fury* drop the *y* before adding -*ious;* and *fame* drops the *e*). Since -*ful* is a suffix that begins with a consonant, the *e* is not dropped in *wasteful* but the *y* in *beauty* changes to an *i*. Talk about how the ending is often misspelled as -*full* because of the meaning connection but assure students that as a suffix it is always spelled with one *l*.

-*ful*	-*ous*	-*ious*	oddball
delightful	**dangerous**	**envious**	outrageous
successful	humorous	studious	
wasteful	mountainous	glorious	
stressful	poisonous	rebellious	
wonderful	vigorous	furious	
shameful	famous		
boastful	scandalous		
cheerful	nervous		
beautiful	marvelous		

Extend

Review the ending -*ness*, -*less*, and -*ly* to see how many words they can be added to from this sort: *cheerfulness, cheerfully, wastefulness, wastefully, nervousness, nervously,* etc. When students do a word hunt encourage them to find more words with compound suffixes.

Additional Words.   *bashful, bountiful, disgraceful, doubtful, fanciful, fearful, grateful, insightful, joyful, meaningful, playful, restful, respectful, scornful, spiteful, suspenseful, tactful, truthful, ungrateful, wistful, youthful, zestful, adventurous, cancerous, continuous, joyous, marvelous, murderous, rigorous, thunderous, torturous, traitorous, treasonous, tremendous, venomous, virtuous, fictitious, gracious, industrious, infectious, laborious, melodious, various, victorious, nauseous, righteous, beauteous*

SORT 13   VERB SUFFIXES (-*EN*, -*IZE*, -*IFY*)

Sort and Reflect

(See page 39.) These derivational suffixes have a similar effect on the base word suggesting "to be or to cause to be," creating verbs (*energize, frighten, terrify*) most of the time, but sometimes adjectives (*forbidden*). Recall from Sort 4 that *en-* is also a prefix and has a similar effect as in *enjoy* or *enclose*. Sort these words first by the suffix and then talk about the meaning of the words as a way to determine the role of the suffix. The words in this sort have base words or obvious roots but some have a spelling change (from *y* to *i* or *e*-drop). Separate out the ones that have a base word ending in *y* or *e* and talk about the generalization that governs the addition of a suffix beginning with a vowel.

-en	-ize	-ify	oddball
frighten	**capitalize**	**classify**	analyze
straighten	civilize	diversify	
dampen	symbolize	falsify	
sweeten	idolize	beautify	
lengthen	visualize	simplify	
forbidden	energize	purify	
mistaken	harmonize		
	memorize		
	summarize		
	apologize		

Extend

Students may confuse the *-ize* and *-yze* endings. Although the *-yze* ending is more common in Great Britain, there is only a handful of words in American English in which /iz/ is spelled *-yze*, and only two that occur with any degree of frequency: *analyze* and *paralyze*. In contrast, hundreds of words end with the *-ize* spelling.

Additional Words.   *broken, darken, deepen, drunken, enlighten, forsaken, frozen, golden, lessen, lighten, outspoken, proven, shaken, sharpen, strengthen, thicken, unbeaten, unbroken, weaken, agonize, alphabetize, brutalize, categorize, customize, crystallize, deodorize, dramatize, fantasize, generalize, glamorize, homogenize, hospitalize, immunize, idealize, magnetize, mobilize, monopolize, organize, pressurize, personalize, popularize, rationalize, scandalize, sensitize, specialize, standardize, tenderize, tranquilize, vandalize, vocalize, vaporize, acidify, clarify, dehumidify, disqualify, electrify, exemplify, glorify, horrify, intensify, mystify, quantify, terrify, versify, paralyze*

REVIEW OF SUFFIXES

Create an activity in which students are given a set of base words (some are listed below) and a set of derivational suffixes (*-er, -est, -ous, -ful, -less, -ness, -ly, -en, -ty, -ize, -ery*) and challenged to match up two parts to create new words. *Prefix Spin* (Chapter 7 of *WTW*), Word Building, or Defiance or Patience (Chapter 8 of *WTW*) can be modified to review suffixes using these words.

> *grace (gracious, graceful, gracefully, graciously)*
> *joy (joyous, joyful, joyfully, joyfulness, joyless, joylessly)*
> *dark (darken, darkness, darkly, darker, darkest)*
> *weak (weakness, weakly, weaker, weakest, weaken)*
> *strange (stranger, strangest, strangely, strangeness)*
> *sensitive (sensitively, sensitivity, sensitize)*
> *tranquil (tranquility, tranquilize, tranquilizer)*
> *real (realist, realistic, reality, really, realize)*
> *brave (braver, bravely, bravest, bravery)*
> *rough (roughness, roughen, rougher, roughest, roughly)*
> *thick (thicker, thickest, thicken, thickly)*

ASSESSMENT 2 FOR SORTS 5–13

Call out the 20 words below for students to spell. Remind them to think about the base word and whether there will be any special spelling change before adding the suffix. You might also ask students to write the base word beside each word.

1. skinny	**2.** agreement	**3.** humidity	**4.** civilian	**5.** inventor
6. laziness	**7.** ordinary	**8.** furious	**9.** mistaken	**10.** earliest
11. politely	**12.** priceless	**13.** directory	**14.** heroic	**15.** memorial
16. merrily	**17.** fearlessness	**18.** marvelous	**19.** idolize	**20.** simplify

SORT 5 Suffixes (-y, -ly, -ily)

-y	*-ly*	*-ily*
scratchy	**silently**	**merrily**
squirmy	velvety	rapidly
secretly	greedily	squeaky
seriously	fluently	hastily
wealthy	skinny	eagerly
readily	swampy	generously
shaggy	politely	silvery
briefly	spotty	bravely

SORT 6   Comparative Suffixes (-*er*, -*est*, -*ier*, -*iest*)

-*er*	-*est*	-*ier*	-*iest*
kinder	**kindest**	**earlier**	
earliest	stranger	emptiest	
cleaner	quieter	trickier	
emptier	cleanest	strangest	
harsher	trickiest	fancier	
crummier	harshest	quietest	
fanciest	shinier	shiniest	
murkier	crummiest	murkiest	

SORT 7   Noun Suffixes (-*er*, -*or*, -*ian*, -*ist*)

-er	*-or*	*-ian*	*-ist*
speaker	**creator**		**guardian**
artist	traveler		visitor
historian	terrorist		finalist
prisoner	decorator		defender
director	Australian		specialist
Asian	believer		inventor
librarian	vocalist		attacker
survivor	admirer		civilian

SORT 8   Suffixes (-*ment*, -*less*, -*ness*)

-*ment*	-*less*	-*ness*
payment	**breathless**	**laziness**
powerlessness	replacement	priceless
blindness	flawless	employment
punishment	dizziness	thoughtless
tactless	agreement	friendliness
politeness	fruitless	amusement
government	emptiness	saltiness
hopeless	fearlessness	

SORT 9   Suffixes (-ary, -ery, -ory)

-ary	-ery	-ory
imaginary	**bravery**	**category**
stationery	library	machinery
lavatory	stationary	mystery
inventory	military	ordinary
scenery	dormitory	victory
history	necessary	century
delivery	February	directory
secretary	January	grocery

SORT 10   Suffixes (-ty, -ity)

baseword	-ty	baseword	-ity
active	**activity**	**safe**	
safety	festive	special	
novelty	tranquil	festivity	
specialty	novel	royal	
casual	royalty	tranquility	
humid	minor	humidity	
certain	casualty	sensitive	
minority	sensitivity	certainty	

SORT 11 Suffixes (-al, -ial, -ic)

-al	*-ial*	*-ic*
fictional	**burial**	**magnetic**
poetic	comical	territorial
accidental	industrial	Islamic
tutorial	arrival	alphabetic
heroic	memorial	logical
patriotic	rhythmic	betrayal
musical	angelic	coastal
editorial	dramatic	global

SORT 12   Adjective Suffixes (-*ful*, -*ous*, -*ious*)

-*ful*	-*ous*	-*ious*
delightful	**dangerous**	**envious**
humorous	successful	poisonous
studious	rebellious	wasteful
stressful	mountainous	famous
vigorous	wonderful	nervous
glorious	marvelous	shameful
cheerful	scandalous	furious
boastful	outrageous	beautiful

SORT 13   Verb Suffixes (-*en*, -*ize*, -*ify*)

-*en*	-*ize*	-*ify*
frighten	**capitalize**	**classify**
civilize	straighten	analyze
diversify	symbolize	dampen
sweeten	falsify	idolize
visualize	lengthen	beautify
simplify	energize	purify
harmonize	forbidden	memorize
summarize	apologize	mistaken

Unit III   The Suffix -ion

NOTES FOR THE TEACHER

Background and Objectives

The suffix *-ion* or /shun/ occurs with considerable frequency and refers to an "action or process" or "the *result* of an action or process" (e.g., if you have an *attraction* for someone, you are *attracted* toward them). Another way to think about it is that adding *-ion* to a word usually changes it from a verb (*decorate*) to a noun (*decoration*). The suffix *-ian* is added to nouns and often suggests someone who "does" (*musician*). The suffix /shun/ can be spelled several ways (*-ion, -tion, -sion, -ian*) and this poses a challenge for spellers. In addition, when it is added to a base, *-ion* often has the effect of "softening" the final consonant sound, as in *select/selection* (where the /t/ sound changes to /sh/) or *music* to *musician* (where the /k/ sound changes to /sh/). Students often remember the various spellings (*-ion, -tion, -sion*), but are uncertain about when to use a particular spelling, and whether and how it affects the spelling of the base word. The generalizations that govern which affix to add and how to add it are reliable but complex. They are covered in a series of sorts in this unit and are also reviewed and extended in later sorts. Hundreds of words end with *-ion*, so spending an extended time with this suffix is worthwhile. Students will:

- Spell the words in these sorts correctly
- Identify base words and the spelling or sound change when the ending is added

Targeted Learners

This unit of study is most appropriate for early derivational relations spellers because it extends the study of suffixes in the previous unit by introducing another common suffix. It continues to prepare students to examine multisyllabic words for base words and affixes. The assessment found on page 46 can be used to determine if students need this unit of study. Students who are able to spell all but one or two words can probably move on to other features.

Teaching Tips

There are many words that end with *-ion* so students will find lots of words when they go on word hunts in just about any reading materials. However, it will be challenging to find words for the specific categories. The list of oddballs may grow very long, but encourage your students to revisit their oddballs after each new sort. By the end of this unit they will be able to find categories for most of them. Working on a large group word hunt chart will help them develop a sense of the most common categories.

   The generalizations that govern how to add *-ion* are complex because they depend upon how the base word ends. You may want to create a generalization chart that you add to with each new sort. However, students are likely to develop a "feel" for these generalizations and there is no reason to expect them to memorize the various conditions. We will list them here for your information.

> Base words that end in two consonants generally add -ion (*subtraction, expression*).
> Base words that end in -ic add -ian (*magician*).
> Base words that end in -te drop the *e* and add -ion (*creation*) or add -ation (*invitation*).
> Base words that end in -de or -d drop the *d/de* and add -sion (*explode* to *explosion*, *expand* to *expansion*).
> Base words that end in -y, drop the *y* and add -action (*satisfy* to *satisfaction*).
> Add -ation when you hear the /a/ sound (as in *adaptation* or *invitation*).
> If in doubt it is probably spelled -tion.

If you desire, you can break this unit into two or three parts and revisit the sorts rather than going through all of them sequentially. You may also want to revise the sorts for students who have more advanced vocabularies by using the words in the additional word list that follows each sort.

The game Stressbusters from Chapter 7 of *WTW* will help to focus attention on accent changes. The activity We Think described in Chapter 8 of *WTW* is designed to review the generalizations covered in this unit.

There are many words in Spanish that end in -*cíon* whose English equivalent ends in -*tion*. In Spanish, the -*cíon* ending is accented, whereas in English the syllable before the ending is accented. Here are just a few examples of obvious cognates: *accíon, anticipacíon, civilizacíon, concentracíon, creacíon, illustracíon, presentacíon.*

SORT 14   ADDING -*ION* TO BASE WORDS, NO SPELLING CHANGE

(See page 48.) The final -*ct* blend is an interesting one. It seldom occurs in one-syllable words (*act, fact,* and *strict* are a few) so it is not usually studied as a blend in earlier stages, but it occurs frequently in words of two or more syllables because it is used to spell a number of Latin stems such as *ject* (*inject*), *tract* (*traction*), *struct* (*construct*) and *duct* (*introduction*). The hard /c/ sound is rather subtle as part of a blend (i.e., *fact* = /fakt/), but the blend "comes apart" when the /shun/ ending is added and the hard c is easier to hear (i.e., *fac-tion* = /fak-shun/).

Demonstrate, Sort, and Reflect

Display a transparency of the words on the overhead or hand out the sheet of words to the students. Ask them what they notice about the words and get ideas about how the words can be sorted. Students usually note that some of the words have familiar prefixes and many end in -*ion*. Tell them that they will be examining the suffix -*ion* and what happens when it is added to base words. Put up the headers and key words and then sort the rest of the words. Begin by sorting the base words by the final letters (-*ct* and -*ss*) under the headers. Then match the affixed word to the base.

The discussion after the sort might go something like this: "Pronounce the words under *collect*. What is the final sound? Now pronounce the words under *collection*. What do you notice about how the base word changes when -*ion* is added?" (The final /t/ sound changes to the sound of /sh/ and the /k/ sound of the *c* is separate and easier to hear.) "Now, pronounce the words under *express* and *expression*. What do you notice about these words when -*ion* is added?" (The final /s/ sound also becomes the sound of /sh/.) Make sure that students understand that there is no change in the spelling of the base word when adding -ion to base words that end in -ct or -ss. Next, discuss the first few base words under collect and express: Beginning with collect, ask the students what the base word means and then ask them what the suffixed word means. Encourage them to put the meanings into their own words. What happens when we put -ion onto a base word? Scaffold their understandings of the following: Putting -ion on a base word results in a word that means "the act or result" of the meaning of the base word. For example, if you collect stamps you have a collection; the act of subtracting one number from another is called the process of subtraction.

base -ct	-tion	base -ss	-sion
collect	collection	express	expression
protect	protection	discuss	discussion
subtract	subtraction	oppress	oppression
select	selection	possess	possession
connect	connection	confess	confession
construct	construction	impress	impression

Additional Words.   abduction, affection, affliction, attraction, convection, destruction, distinction, extinction, election, eviction, instruction, malfunction, perfection, prediction, production, reflection, rejection, compression, depression, digression, obsession, profession, procession, regression, recession

Extend

When students go on word hunts they will find many words that end with -ion that do not fit either the ct or the ss category. At this point help the students identify words that come from base words that end in either -ct or -ss and have them add those to their word study notebooks. Other words ending in -tion will go into the miscellaneous category for now. Students can refer to their lists as they add more categories in the sorts that follow and put those words into the appropriate categories.

SORT 15   ADDING -ION AND -IAN, NO SPELLING CHANGE

(See page 49.) The -ian suffix has been studied earlier in Sort 7 but it is revisited here where the sound is distinctly /shun/ and it is added to words that end in -ic.

Demonstrate, Sort, and Reflect

Introduce this sort in the same manner as Sort 14. After the students have noted the base word/suffixed word distinction, discuss the base + -ion pattern, examining the suffix -ion and what happens to the sound of t when it is added to the base words. Remind the students that last week they looked at words ending in -ct. Ask them what they notice about these words (they also end in a consonant +t and -ion is simply added). As with -ct, the blend is split with the addition of the ending and it is sometimes easier to hear the two sounds (ex-cept becomes ex-cep-tion).

Then, have students examine the base word + -ian pattern and how the sound of the c changes. Facilitate their discussion of how -ian is different from -ion: -ian usually refers to a specialist or person who does something, as in magician (more broadly, "relating to, belonging to, or resembling").

base -t	-ion	base -ic	-ian
invent	**invention**	**magic**	**magician**
digest	digestion	music	musician
desert	desertion	electric	electrician
suggest	suggestion	clinic	clinician
adopt	adoption		
insert	insertion		
distort	distortion		
prevent	prevention		

Additional Words.   *abortion, assertion, congestion, disruption, interruption, proportion, indigestion, exhaustion, eruption, exception, desertion, beautician, dietician, diagnostician, logician, mortician, optician, obstetrician, pediatrician, politician, physician, statistician, technician*

Extend

Identify where the accent falls in the words ending with -t (the final syllable) by reading down the list. Then read the words where the -ion has been added to find that the accent does not change—the accent falls on the syllable right before the suffix. Then read the words that end in -ic. These words are accented on the first syllable and when -ian is added the accent shifts to the next syllable.

In a word hunt students need to think about the base word (does it end in -t or -ic) before adding it to their lists. There are many words ending in -ian whose meaning suggests "relating to, belonging to, or resembling" and students might revisit their word hunt from Sort 7 to see if there are any words there that can be added to the category of words whose base ends in -ic.

SORT 16   ADDING -ION, E-DROP, AND SPELLING CHANGE

Demonstrate, Sort, and Reflect

(See page 50.) In this sort all the base words end with -e. The e is simply dropped after t, but in the case of words ending in -de, the d is changed to t before adding -ion. Have the students sort the base words into two categories. They will probably notice that the words have different endings: Some end in -de and others end in -t. Next, have the students match each base word with its suffixed form. Ask them what happens when -ion is added to each group? Read down each column to focus attention on the sound change. Students might detect a slight sound difference between -tion /shun/ and -sion /zhun/. The /zhun/ sound is "voiced" just as the /d/ sound is voiced (i.e., the vocal chords vibrate) as compared to the "unvoiced" /t/ and /shun/.

Have them record these sorts in their vocabulary notebooks and write a "rule" in their own words. When adding -ion to words that end in -de, drop the de and add -sion. If necessary, mention that, just as with the words in the previous sort, they should pay attention to whether the sound of the base word changes when a suffix is added.

You may wish to ask the students if they see a base word within *decorate*. Ask them if they've heard of the word *décor* before. Discuss its meaning.

base -*te*	e-drop + *ion*	base -*de/d*	d > *sion*
operate	**operation**	**explode**	**explosion**
create	creation	erode	erosion
decorate	decoration	allude	allusion
illustrate	illustration	invade	invasion
imitate	imitation	conclude	conclusion
		comprehend	comprehension
		expand	expansion

Additional Words.   *congratulation, circulation, devotion, dictation, donation, education, frustration, generation, graduation, hesitation, hibernation, isolation, indication, location, migration, pollution, translation, vacation, vibration, collision, delusion, division, evasion, erosion, inclusion, intrusion, persuasion, protrusion, provision, seclusion, apprehension, suspension, extension, intension, suspension*

Extend

Read word lists for patterns of stress. The accent shifts in the words ending in -*te* but not with the words ending in -*de*.

Talk about the suffix -*ate*. Generally it signals verbs and there are hundreds of them. It was not studied in the second unit because it is usually added to roots (*animate*) but rarely added to base words (*captivate*). Pull out the words in this sort that end in -*ate* (*operate, create, decorate*, etc.) and talk about how they are all action verbs. Add -*ate* to the chart of suffixes and have students hunt for more words that end in -*ate*. Watch out for homographs such as *associate, duplicate*, and *graduate* that can be both a verb or a noun depending on the pronunciation of the final syllable: When you *graduate* (long *a*) you become a *graduate* (schwa sound or short *i*).

SORT 17   ADDING -*ATION*, -*CATION*, AND -*ITION*

Demonstrate, Sort, and Reflect

(See page 51.) Often -*ation*, and sometimes -*cation* and -*ition*, are added to verbs to change them into nouns. They usually pose few problems for the speller because they can hear the stressed long *a* in -*ation* and the short *i* in -*ition*. In this sort, four cases are examined without the base words. Words that simply add -*ation*, those that drop the *e* before adding -*ation*, those that change from *y* to *i* and add -*cation*, and those that add -*ition*.

Display the four key words for this sort: *information, organization, application*, and *addition*. Identify the base word in each one and talk about what has been added (-*ation*, -*cation*, or -*ition*) and the spelling change where *y* is changed to *i*. Add the headers as each is discussed (-*ation*, e-drop, -*cation*, -*ition*) and talk about the meaning of both the base word and derived word. Compare to the discoveries in previous sorts (*collection, expression, operation*) to determine that these affixes work the same way to change verbs to nouns that mean the act of or process of. However, by adding -*ation* there is no change in the final consonant sound of the base word. Compare *operation* to *presentation*. Sort the rest of the words with the student's help, encouraging them to think about the base word before sorting and talking about the meaning of each. After sorting, read the words in columns and focus attention on the sound in accented syllables. Students should be able to hear the difference in words that end with *-ation* and *-ition*.

When students work with their own words you can have them underline or write the base above or below the word on their cards or in their word study notebooks since the base words are not included for comparison in this sort. Talk about how the sound shifts in words that end with *y* from long *i* to short *i* along with the change in spelling. This idea that vowel sounds alternate as endings are added will be explored in the next unit.

-ation	e-drop	-cation	-ition
information	**organization**	**application**	**addition**
consideration	imagination	identification	partition
presentation	reservation	justification	edition
relaxation	starvation	purification	
temptation	quotation	beautification	
transportation	examination	gratification	
expectation	memorization	notification	

Additional Words.

(no change) *annexation, carbonation, confirmation, floatation, importation, indentation, liqui-dation, lamentation, plantation, recommendation, ruination, transformation, vexation*

(e-drop) *authorization, capitalization, civilization, combination, conservation, conversation, determination, observation, exploration, invitation, inspiration, perspiration, prepara-tion, preservation, realization, visualization*

(change y to i and add -cation) *certification, electrification, falsification, glorification, mag-nification, pacification, qualification, ratification, simplification, unification, verification*

(add -ition) *abolition, competition, composition, definition, demolition, exposition, ignition, preposition, prohibition, recognition*

Extend

When students go on word hunts they now have a number of categories of base words to consider when they come across words that end in *-ion*. When students find words in which the spelling of the base changes when the suffix is added, have them record these words in a "miscellaneous" category, but ask them to keep their eyes open for a pattern in these words as well. In later sorts "predictable spelling changes" such as *receive* to *reception* or *permit* to *permission* will be addressed.

ASSESSMENT 3 FOR SORTS 14–17

Review, Retention, and Transfer

Write the following base words on the board: *collect, express, invent, magic, explode, operate, organize, inform, apply,* and *add.* Have students explain the spelling and sound changes that occur when /shun/ is added to each one and write the derived word.

Call out the first 10 words on page 47 and ask students to spell them. Remind students to think about the base word. All of these words have been studied during this unit. To check understanding of word meanings, you may wish to have the students write sentences using them.

Next write the base words in the next 10 words on the board and ask students to add the /shun/ ending to each. Do not pronounce the derived word in parentheses but see if students can generate it themselves. These words have not been studied in the sorts in this unit but will assess for transfer of the spelling generalizations.

Retention Words

1. selection
2. starvation
3. adoption
4. musician
5. relaxation
6. impression
7. imitation
8. erosion
9. notification
10. partition

Transfer Words

1. attract (attraction)
2. depress (depression)
3. erupt (eruption)
4. optic (optician)
5. collide (collision)
6. graduate (graduation)
7. extend (extension)
8. carbon (carbonation)
9. define (definition)
10. explore (exploration)

SORT 14   Adding *-ion* to Base Words, No Spelling Change

base -ct	*-tion*	*-sion*	*base -ss*
collect		**collection**	**express**
expression		protect	discuss
protection		subtraction	select
construct		connect	oppress
selection		possess	subtract
confession		connection	construction
oppression		impress	possession
discussion		confess	impression

SORT 15   Adding *-ion* and *-ian*, No Spelling Change

base -t	-ion	-ian	base -ic
invent	**invention**		**magic**
magician	digest		suggest
adoption	insertion		desert
electric	suggestion		prevention
digestion	musician		clinic
music	adopt		desertion
distort	electrician		prevent
insert	clinician		distortion

SORT 16   Adding -ion, e-Drop, and Spelling Change

base -te	e-drop + ion	base -de/d	d > sion
operate		operation	explode
explosion	create		erosion
invade	conclusion		decorate
expand	creation		comprehend
allude	illustration		erode
decoration	invasion		imitation
conclude	comprehension		illustrate
imitate	expansion		allusion

SORT 17   Adding -ation, -cation, and -ition

-ation	e-drop	-cation	-ition
information	**organization**		**application**
addition	consideration		relaxation
temptation	identification		imagination
partition	transportation		expectation
reservation	presentation		edition
starvation	memorization		quotation
purification	beautification		justification
notification	examination		gratification

Unit IV Vowel and Consonant Alternations

NOTES FOR THE TEACHER

Background and Objectives

In these sorts students will explicitly explore the spelling-meaning connection through the examination of vowel and consonant *alternations*. The term *alternation* refers to the sound changes that occur across words that are related in spelling and meaning. In Sort 18, for example, the silent consonant in one word in a spelling-meaning pair is sounded in the related word (*sign/signature*); in Sort 19, the long vowel in one word alternates with a short vowel in the related word (*nature/natural*). The *spelling*, however, changes little if at all—and this is the essence of the *spelling-meaning connection:* **Words that are related in meaning are often related in spelling as well, despite changes in sound.** Student understanding of this connection is an important strategy: When uncertain how to spell a particular word, students should try to think of another word that is related in terms of spelling and meaning, and it will usually provide a clue. The *spelling-meaning connection* also supports vocabulary development: If students understand one word in a spelling-meaning family of words, they usually can learn the meanings of the related words. The similar spelling of words in a spelling-meaning family visually represents the meaning relationships that they share. Students will:

- Identify consonants and vowels that alternate in related words
- Demonstrate understanding of prefixes, suffixes, and base words
- Spell the words in this unit and demonstrate an understanding of their meaning

Targeted Learners

These sorts are for students in the middle derivational relations stage who are familiar with many prefixes and suffixes. The words chosen for these sorts are ones that students in middle school might be expected to know. If you are working with students with more advanced vocabularies there are usually additional words listed that can be substituted for easier words. The assessment on page 61 can be used as a pretest to determine which students will benefit the most from these sorts. Students who misspell only one or two words can move to later units or you may just use Sorts 22 and 24 as a review.

Teaching Tips

The list of standard weekly routines on pages 5–6 will give you ideas about how to engage students in meaningful extensions to the introductory sorting lesson. Because these words have systematic sound changes, blind sorts are useful to do with partners. Word hunts, however, will be difficult for the features of study in this unit because alternations are often not obvious until pairs are put side by side. Instead, students can be assigned dictionary work in which they look up pairs of words (three to five pairs at a time) to see how they are represented phonetically. This will help students learn how to use dictionaries as a guide to pronunciation. Of course they can also look up the meanings of words, especially those that might not be familiar or words that have multiple meanings.

You may find it helpful to develop a system for marking vowels and stress as you work with these words to draw attention to the way sounds and stress alternate in pairs of words. Vowels may be marked as long (macron/⁻) or short (breve/˘) or with a schwa(ə). Stressed syllables might be indicated with accent marks or be underlined. Check the dictionaries you will be using to see how accent and the schwa sound are represented. Some dictionaries use bold letters to indicate stress and the letter *u* instead of the schwa symbol. Dictionaries do not always agree on pronunciation. This is particularly true with respect to unaccented syllables. For example, the *American Heritage Dictionary* lists the boldfaced vowel in *humid* as a short *-i*; *Merriam-Webster* lists it as a schwa.

Identifying the accented syllable can sometimes be hard for students as well as teachers. It is not important whether students gain mastery over this skill and it need not be assessed. However, attention to accent or stress not only helps spellers but it can also help ELLs who are learning to pronounce English. Pair up ELLs to work with native speakers of English who can model pronunciation.

The words in this unit offer opportunities to review the prefixes and suffixes covered in earlier sorts and if you created charts in previous units they will get plenty of use. Take the time to talk about how the suffixes affect the meaning and usage of a word as well as the sound alternations that are the foci of these lessons.

SORT 18   CONSONANT ALTERNATION

(See page 62.) This sort provides an excellent opportunity to introduce students explicitly to the relationship between spelling and meaning. The meaning connection between most of the words in this sort is fairly straightforward. Sometimes, however, this relationship is not as apparent—as, for example, between *design* and *designate*. This is a good opportunity to refer students to the etymological information for *design* and *designate* in the dictionary; both words come from a Latin term that means "to mark." When someone is *designated* as a spokesperson, for example, she or he is in a sense "marked" to perform this duty (such as a *designated* driver). When an architect *designs* a house, she is "marking" how the house will be laid out and how it will look.

Demonstrate, Sort, and Reflect

You may introduce the sort by saying to the students, as you write on the board, "When I *sign* my name [write *sign* on the board] I include a *g* even though I do not hear it. I've just given you a clue as to *why* there's a *g* in the word *sign*." If the students do not respond, prompt them with, "When you sign a letter, what is that called?" [*Signature*] "Do you hear the sound of the *g* now?" Write up *signature* under the word *sign* and underline the *g* in both words. Follow this up by writing *muscle* on the board. "What letter is silent in this word? Is there a word related in spelling and meaning to *muscle* and in which the *c* is pronounced?" [*Muscular*] Write *muscular* underneath *muscle* and underline the *c* in both words. Explain to the students that words related in meaning are often related in spelling as well, despite changes in sound. Thinking of a related word may help students remember how to spell another word.

Set up *sign* and *signature* as headers and model how to sort pairs of words. Ask students which pair has a silent letter and place it under *sign*. Continue sorting all of the words with the students' help.

Silent consonant	Sounded consonant	Silent consonant	Sounded consonant
sign	**signature**	column	columnist
bomb	bombard	hymn	hymnal
soften	soft	resign	resignation
muscle	muscular	hasten	haste
crumb	crumble	solemn	solemnity
design	designate	moisten	moist

Extend

Give students their own set of words to pair up and have them underline the consonants that alternate in each pair. See the list of standard weekly routines on pages 5–6 for further extensions but do not expect students to find more of these words in a word hunt.

The words in this sort offer possibilities for suffix review. Ask students to identify words with suffixes in the derived words (*hymnal, designate, solemnity, columnist, resignation*) and talk about their meanings and/or their effect of the suffix on the base to which they are attached.

Additional Words.   allege/allegation, autumn/autumnal, condemn/condemnation, debt/debit, damn/damnation, fasten/fast, malign/malignant, paradigm/paradigmatic

SORT 19   VOWEL ALTERNATION: LONG TO SHORT

(See page 63.) This sort focuses on the constancy of spelling despite a change in pronunciation of the vowel from the base to its derived word or its *derivative*, a word that comes from or is *derived* from the base. (This is an appropriate place in word study at the derivational level to begin to use these terms with students.)

Demonstrate, Sort, and Reflect

Ask the students how they might sort the words. They will probably notice that some are base words. Suggest that they sort the words into base words and related suffixed or *derived* words. After the related words have been matched up, read each pair of words and ask the students to listen to the sound of the vowel in the accented syllable. You may want to mark the vowels with macrons (¯) and breves (˘). Discuss how the spelling of the word does not change even in words like *breath* and *pleasant*. Remind the students that this is because the words are related in meaning; this is the spelling-meaning connection. Because *please* is related to *pleasant* in meaning (a *pleasant* person tries to *please*), the spelling of the base words remains the same.

Take time to talk about the meaning of the words. Words like *type* and *mine* have several meanings and it is important to talk about the one that is related to the derived word. For example, *mine* refers to a place in which minerals are extracted or dug out, not to the possessive pronoun. Several of the words end in -*al* which suggests "of," or "related to" or "associated with." A **criminal** is someone associated with **crime**.

Long vowel	Short vowel	Long vowel	Short vowel
please	**pleasant**	athlete	athletic
mine	mineral	type	typical
breathe	breath	crime	criminal
revise	revision	humane	humanity
nature	natural	ignite	ignition
cave	cavity	precise	precision

Extend

Give students their own set of words to match up. Students can be asked to mark the vowels as they write the pairs in their word study notebook. Students can also sort the base words by the long vowel sound (long *a*, *i*, and *e*).

Additional Words. *convene/convention, episode/episodic, extreme/extremity, grave/gravity, grateful/ gratitude, page/paginate, profane/profanity, reptile/reptilian, rite/ritual, televise/ television, telescope/telescopic*

SORT 20   VOWEL ALTERNATION: LONG TO SHORT OR SCHWA

(See page 64.) The words in this sort help students contrast the long/short vowel alternation pattern with a schwa. Many spelling errors at this level are in the unaccented syllables of words, so these spelling-meaning patterns are helpful to study. In addition, this sort will help students attend to accent within words.

Demonstrate and Sort

Introduce the sort by asking the students if they've ever had to stop and think about how to spell a particular word, such as *competition* or *admiration*. Tell them that thinking of a related word may provide a clue. For example, thinking of the base word *compete* will help with spelling the word *competition*; thinking of the base word *admire* may help with *admiration*. Tell them that this is one of the spelling-meaning patterns they are going to explore in these words.

Have the students match up each base word with its derivative. Begin the next step of the sort by reviewing the long to short alternation in key words *volcano* and *volcanic*. Put these under the headers long and short. Then compare *compose* and *composition*. Identify the long /o/ sound in the accented syllable of *compose*. Then ask students what sound the *o* has in the word *composition*. Does the long *o* in *composition* change to a short *o* in *composition*? Not exactly. In *volcanic*, the second syllable is clearly accented—in other words, it gets most of the "oomph" when we say the word. In *composition*, is the second syllable clearly accented? No. Because the second syllable is not accented, the vowel sound in the second syllable of *composition* sounds like a schwa/ə/, an unaccented short /ŭ/ sound, because there's no "oomph" behind it. Put the key words under the headers and then sort the rest of the words according to whether the long vowel alternates with a short sound or the schwa. Read each pair and help students identify the stressed syllable. The long to short pairs will not have a change in accent but the long to schwa pairs will change. Underline the accented syllable in each pair.

Reflect

Point to the schwa sound in *composition, competition,* and *invitation* and ask students what vowel spells the schwa sound (*o*, *e*, and *i*). Explain that this is what makes these words hard to spell. Sound is not a clue to the vowel. Ask them what will offer a clue to the vowel (thinking of a related word in which the vowel is heard). You might present a misspelling (*oppisition*, for example) and ask students what word would clear up the spelling of the schwa sound and why. Have students look up several of the derived words to see how the schwa and stress are represented in their dictionary.

Talk about the meaning of the paired words and how the meanings are related. Discuss how *custodian* refers not just to an individual who maintains the condition of a school; it has a broader application, referring to anyone who holds custody of something, including an idea—as, for example, when a people are referred to as "*custodians of democracy.*"

Long vowel	Short vowel	Long vowel	Schwa
volcano	**volcanic**	**compose**	**composition**
conspire	conspiracy	compete	competition
serene	serenity	admire	admiration
divine	divinity	custodian	custody
		define	definition
		invite	invitation
		reside	resident
		oppose	opposition

Extend

After students record the sort in their word study notebook, ask them to underline the accented syllables to reinforce the idea that accent sometimes changes with the addition of suffixes. If they are uncertain where the accent falls let them work with partners (this is especially important for ELLs who may need help pronouncing the words) and use the dictionary.

Students may begin to notice and comment on relationships that do not appear to make sense in terms of spelling and meaning. For example, are *admiral* and *admire* related? These words actually come from different languages and are not related in meaning. *Admire* comes from French in which it means "to wonder" (and is related to *miracle* and *miraculous*, which also have to do with "wonder"); *admiral* comes from an Arabic word for "commander." Occasionally, exceptions such as these do occur. Exploring the history or etymology of the terms usually reveals the disconnect.

Additional Words.

> **Long to short** *convene/convention, flame/flammable, episode/episodic, know/knowledge, precocious/precocity, produce/production, reptile/reptilian, sane/sanity, senile/senility*
> **Long to schwa** *combine/combination, comedian/comedy, compile/compilation, deprive/deprivation, expose/exposition, explore/exploration, famous/infamous, impose/imposition, incline/inclination, perspire/perspiration, narrate/narrative, native/nativity, pose/position, recite/recitation, relate/relative, stable/stability*

SORT 21   ADDING SUFFIX -*ITY*: VOWEL ALTERNATION, SCHWA TO SHORT

(See page 65.) Students first dealt with the suffix -*ity* (meaning "state" or "quality") when it was introduced in Sort 10, and with the -*al* ending in Sort 11 where students learned that it often signals an adjective. In this sort, the unaccented final syllable in each base word becomes accented when -*ity* is affixed and the vowel sound alternates from schwa to short.

Words that end in -*dad* are quite common in Spanish. They usually correspond to an English word that ends in -*ity*: *autoridad* (*authority*), *necesidad* (*necessity*), *universidad* (*university*), *formalidad* (*formality*), *velocidad* (*velocity*).

Demonstrate, Sort, and Reflect

Ask the students how they might sort the words. An obvious suggestion is to put the -*ity* words together in one column and their related words in the other column. Ask the students to look at the first few word pairs. What do they notice when -*ity* is added? Using *personal* and *personality* as examples, discuss how accent affects the vowel sounds. In **per**sonal, the first syllable is accented and there is a schwa sound in the final unaccented syllable. In *perso**nal**ity*, the accent shifts to the third syllable and the vowel sound is short. Then talk about the meaning and usage of each word and the suffixes. *Personal* is an adjective ending in -*al* that is changed to a noun with the addition of -*ity*. Discuss several more words in this same fashion.

-əl	-ity	-əl	-ity
personal	**personality**	local	locality
hostile	hostility	mobile	mobility
mental	mentality	formal	formality
fatal	fatality	fertile	fertility
general	generality	original	originality
brutal	brutality	individual	individuality

Extend

Ask students to find the three base words that end in -*ile* and talk about how the *e* is dropped before the suffix -*ity* because it begins with a vowel. *Mobile* and *hostile* have alternative pronunciations so this is a good time to examine how they are represented in a dictionary. The word *mobile* is a homograph with several meanings so take time to examine them all.

Ask the students if they have ever heard someone described as having a *genial* personality. How might *genial* be spelled? If they are uncertain—or even if they aren't—ask the students to listen to the following description to see if it provides a clue: "Suzette has a *genial* personality. She is outgoing and supportive, and always wants to know if there is anything she can do for you. Suzette's *geniality* is the most likable aspect of her." Knowing that the vowel sound in the derived word *geniality* is clearly short will help the student know that the unaccented, and therefore ambiguous, final syllable in *genial* is spelled with -*al*.

Students should be able to find lots of words that end in -*ity* on a word hunt, although some of them, unlike the words in this sort, will not end in -*lity*. They might revisit the word hunt they did for Sort 10 and see if there are any words that end in -*lity*. As an alternative to sentence writing, ask students to find a noun that can be described by the adjectives ending in -*al* (*mental arithmetic, formal dance, local plants*, etc.).

Additional Words.   *actuality, centrality, eventuality, finality, frugality, hospitality, legality, musicality, modality, morality, mortality, neutrality, normality, partiality, practicality, probability, punctuality, sexuality, spirituality, technicality, totality, tranquility, triviality, vitality,* (ile) *facility, fragility, gentility, infertility, nobility, senility, stability, sterility, versatility*

SORT 22   VOWEL ALTERNATIONS: LONG, SHORT, AND SCHWA

Demonstrate, Sort, and Reflect

(See page 66.) In this sort students will review the three vowel alternations. Put up the headers and the three key word pairs. Talk about each one in turn. Listen to *suffice.*

What is the vowel sound in the accented syllable? What happens to the long-vowel sound in the word *sufficient*? Repeat with *preside* and *president* where the vowel in the accented syllable changes from long to schwa. In the case of *metallic*, the accented vowel is short *a* and in *metal* the *a* changes to the schwa sound while the accent changes to the first syllable.

An alternative way to begin this sort if you have a large group is to give each student one word and let students move around the room to find the person with the related word to make a pair. Working in partners they should decide where their pair should go and explain their reason for the rest of the class when they come up to sort it.

This sort presents several opportunities for extending students' vocabulary by having the students sort the words into base words and derived words. Students will be familiar with *sufficient*, but may not know *suffice*. Have the students discuss what *sufficient* means, giving examples. Based on the meaning of *sufficient*, therefore, what might *suffice* mean? Both *impede* and *impediment* are probably new terms, so scaffold students' understanding with examples that follow the guidelines on page 4.

Long to short		Long to schwa		Short to schwa	
suffice	**sufficient**	**preside**	**president**	**metallic**	**metal**
democrat	democracy	inspire	inspiration	emphatic	emphasis
wise	wisdom	mandate	mandatory	habit	habitat
decide	decision	narrate	narrative	excel	excellent

Extend

Point out the spelling of *excel* and *excellent*. Ask students why the *l* doubled before adding *-ent* (it is a suffix beginning with a vowel). Review the suffixes studied in earlier sorts (*-ment, -ion, -ic*). You may wish to have the students do a "part of speech" sort with these words.

You may want to take some time to examine other words that end like *democrat* and *democracy*. The suffixes *-crat* and *-cracy* mean "rule or government" and can be found in words like *autocrat, aristocrat, bureaucrat*. The suffixes *-arch* and *-archy* also mean "rule" and occur in *monarchy, anarchy, matriarchy*, and *patriarch*.

Additional Words.   *comedian/comedy, declare/declaration, derive/derivation, democratic/ democracy, emphatic/emphasis, geometry/geometric, harmonious/harmony, illustrate/illustrative, impede/impediment, labor/laborious, major/majority, mediocre/mediocrity, period/periodic, precocious/precocity, produce/production, specific/specify*

SORT 23   ADDING -*ION*: VOWEL ALTERNATION, SPELLING CHANGE

(See page 67.) This sort examines words in which the spelling of the vowel pattern within the base changes when a suffix is added. Note that, although this change in spelling is an exception to the spelling-meaning connection, it is an exception that nonetheless follows a pattern; that is, when spelling *does* change within a spelling-meaning family of words, it does so *predictably*. There is a *pattern*, in other words, that occurs across words of a certain type, and a number of words usually follow this pattern.

Demonstrate, Sort, and Reflect

Have students sort the words by matching up base words with derived words and then sort by the ending (-*ation* or -*ption*). Talk about the alternation in vowel sound from long to short when the ending is added. Then ask students what they notice about the patterns in the base word and the spelling changes before adding /shun/. You may tell the students that, although there are only a few instances of these particular patterns, you are addressing it to point out that, even when words appear odd, there are almost always other words that follow that same pattern.

Discuss the meanings of any unfamiliar words and help students recall that verbs are changed to nouns with the addition of the -*ion* suffix. Many students will struggle with the spelling of *perceive* and *receive* because of the unusual *ei* pattern. This may be a good place to review the jingle "*i* before *e* except after *c*." Brainstorm other words that work like this, such as *ceiling*.

base *-ai-*	derived *-ation*	base *-e*	derived *-ption*
exclaim	**exclamation**	**assume**	**assumption**
proclaim	proclamation	presume	presumption
acclaim	acclamation	consume	consumption
explain	explanation	resume	resumption
reclaim	reclamation	receive	reception
		perceive	perception

Extend

If you created a chart earlier during the -*ion* unit you may want to add to it based on this sort. The new generalization should say something like this: "Certain word patterns change their spelling in predictable ways before adding -*tion*: *exclaim* to *exclamation*, *assume* to *assumption*, *receive* to *reception*."

More examples can be added as they are studied in later sorts. For example, words with the Latin stem *scribe* will change to *script* before -*ion* as in *prescribe/prescription*, and *tain* will change to *ten* as in *maintain/maintenance*.

Additional Words.   *maintain/maintenance, abstain/abstinence, retain/retention, absorb/absorption, conceive/conception*

SORT 24   MULTIPLE ALTERNATIONS

Demonstrate, Sort, and Reflect

(See page 68.) There are no headers for this sort. Rather than sorting the words into columns and matching base words and derived words, have students sort words according to spelling-meaning families, putting words that they believe go together in groups. (This is because in some groupings, such as *physics/physicist*, there doesn't appear to be a base word—*physics* without the *s* does not really work here!) Have students examine their groupings, and ask them what they notice. Name the words in each spelling-meaning family and discuss how the words are related in meaning and how the suffixes signal the part of speech. You may wish to point out that *politics*, *political*, and *politician* come from the Greek word *polis*, which means "city." In classical Greece, the *city* was the primary form of government, not the nation or country.

For each spelling-meaning family, have students work singly or in pairs to see how many types of vowel and consonant alternations occur. Look across all of the words, and then group together the words in which there is a long/short vowel alternation (e.g., *nation/national*). Next, group words in which there is short/schwa alternation (e.g., *critic/critical*). Are there words in which more than one type of vowel alternation is occurring? (Yes, for example, **pol**itics/**pol**itical/**pol**itician.) Group together words in which the sound of the consonant changes, but the spelling stays the same (e.g., *critic/criticize, except/exception*).

critic	public	physics	nation
critical	publicize	physical	national
criticize	publicity	physicist	nationality
politics	except	family	spirit
political	exception	familiar	spiritual
politician	exceptional	familiarity	spirituality

Extend

Students can be asked to identify word families in which the accent changes with the addition of suffixes. Challenge students to use all three words in a sentence that demonstrates their understanding and usage of the words: *A physicist is a scientist who studies physics or things in the physical world.*

Additional Words.   *celebrate, celebration, celebrity, comic, comical, comedy, comedian, divert, diversion, diversity, diplomat, diplomatic, diplomacy, office, official, officiate, obsolete, obsolescence, punish, punitive, impunity, reciprocate, reciprocity, reciprocal, romance, romantic, romanticize, rhapsody, rhapsodic, specify, specific, specificity*

ASSESSMENT 4 FOR SORTS 18–24

Ask students to spell and define the following 15 words. Remind them to think of derivationally related words in which the sounds may be more clear.

1. design
2. moisten
3. typical
4. competition
5. opposition
6. fertile
7. mobility
8. sufficient
9. receive
10. emphasis
11. publicity
12. politician
13. narrative
14. consumption
15. proclaim

SORT 18   Consonant Alternation

silent consonant	*sounded consonant*	
sign	**signature**	bomb
soften	muscular	design
crumb	columnist	hymnal
muscle	bombard	soft
resign	crumble	hasten
designate	hymn	column
haste	solemn	moisten
solemnity	moist	resignation

SORT 19   Vowel Alternation: Long to Short

long vowel	*short vowel*	
please	**pleasant**	mineral
breathe	revision	cavity
mine	athletic	breath
revise	humanity	nature
athlete	natural	cave
precise	criminal	humane
type	ignition	typical
crime	precision	ignite

SORT 20   Vowel Alternation: Long to Short or Schwa

long vowel	short vowel	long vowel	schwa
volcano	**volcanic**		**compose**
composition	conspire		admire
custodian	competition		serene
divine	conspiracy		custody
compete	admiration		invitation
define	serenity		divinity
invite	opposition		definition
reside	oppose		resident

SORT 21   Adding Suffix -ity: Vowel Alternation, Schwa to Short

-əl	-ity	
personal	**personality**	hostile
brutal	mentality	general
hostility	fatality	mental
fatal	formality	local
mobile	generality	brutality
locality	original	formal
individual	originality	mobility
fertile	individuality	fertility

SORT 22   Vowel Alternations: Long, Short, and Schwa

long to short	long to schwa	short to schwa
suffice	**sufficient**	**preside**
president	**metallic**	**metal**
wise	inspiration	emphasis
mandate	emphatic	inspire
democrat	wisdom	decide
excel	mandatory	narrate
decision	narrative	democracy
habit	excellent	habitat

SORT 23   Adding -ion: Vowel Alternation, Spelling Change

base -ai-	-ation	base -e	-ption
exclaim	**exclamation**	**assume**	
assumption	proclamation	explain	
presume	reclamation	proclaim	
acclaim	consumption	reclaim	
perceive	acclamation	resume	
receive	explanation	reception	
consume	presumption	resumption	
	perception		

SORT 24   Multiple Alternations

critic	publicize	except
politics	criticize	physics
publicity	public	critical
exception	political	nation
family	physical	familiarity
physicist	exceptional	spirit
national	familiar	nationality
spiritual	politician	spirituality

Unit V   Greek and Latin Elements I

NOTES FOR THE TEACHER

Background and Objectives

In these sorts we begin the more systematic and formal exploration of Greek and Latin elements and their combinations. Literally thousands of English words are derived from Greek and Latin and the generative nature of English becomes evident in the study of these elements. Often, when we need a new term, especially when we need scientific names, we go back to these elements. Students who are taking biology and other content subjects are likely to encounter hundreds of words such as these, and an understanding of how Latin and Greek elements work will help with the vocabulary load they need to acquire.

When discussing meaningful elements in words that are neither prefixes nor suffixes, linguists make a terminological distinction between elements that come from Latin and elements that come from Greek. Stems, roots, and combining forms are all used, but it is not necessary to make this distinction with students; the term **root** usually works well enough for both Greek and Latin elements and is widely used. See Chapter 8 in *WTW* for a fuller discussion of these terms.

We begin with number and size prefixes and their combination with bases and roots. Then we move to Greek roots because they occur fairly frequently in printed materials from the intermediate grades onward *and* their meaning is also relatively concrete and straightforward. The systematic exploration of Latin roots will begin with Sort 30, beginning with the most common and transparent roots. The spelling of some Latin roots changes across related words. We have both *flexible* and *reflect* in which the roots (*flex* and *flect*) mean "bend." We have both *inscribe* and *transcript* in which the roots (*scribe* and *script*) mean "write." These forms come from the original Latin verbs, in which the sound changed in different forms, and therefore the spelling changed as well. This is similar to what happens in many English verbs: We *come* to visit today / we *came* to visit yesterday; I will *run* quickly / I *ran* quickly. Students will:

- Learn to identify the Greek and Latin elements in polysyllabic words
- Find or brainstorm additional words that share the same elements
- Spell and demonstrate an understanding of the meaning of words, prefixes, and roots covered in these sorts

Targeted Learners

These sorts are appropriate for students in the middle to late derivational relations stage who are familiar with prefixes and suffixes. The assessments found at the end of this unit can be used as both pretests and posttests but nearly all students at all levels (including adults!) will benefit from the study of these Greek and Latin elements. The words selected for these sorts are appropriate for upper elementary and middle school students. For secondary students you might substitute less common words listed under the additional words for each sort.

These sorts will systematically cover many Greek and Latin elements; however, the sorts can be used out of sequence at any time depending on your curricular needs. For example, if you are studying geometric shapes you might want to use the sort dealing with number prefixes.

The selection and sequencing of roots is based on their semantic transparency and the types of elements with which they combine. (See Chapter 8 in *WTW* for further explanation of scope and sequence.) At this phase of word study during the derivational relations stage, students will continue to explore base word/derived word spelling-meaning patterns. This is also the point, however, at which more focused exploration of Greek and Latin word elements can begin—thus the inclusion of these sorts at this point in the scope and sequence of word study.

Teaching Tips

Throughout this unit you will want students to find other words that share the same elements and to add these to their word study notebooks. Encourage students to continue to look for featured roots over time rather than just the week in which particular roots are studied. It may be easier to brainstorm words than to actually find them in reading materials because the words become far less common as we progress through this unit of study. As mentioned before, words with prefixes are easy to find in dictionaries, but when the element comes later in the word it is a challenge. Searching online dictionaries such as www.yourdictionary.com with the use of an asterisk (e.g., *spec*) can turn up additional words; another excellent word and pattern search website is www.onelook.com.

Dictionaries should be used regularly throughout this unit and students should learn how to look for and interpret the etymological information that is often provided at the end of a definition. Not all dictionaries have eytomologies, so have at least one on hand in the classroom that does. An online etymological dictionary can be found at www.etymonline.com/. There are other resources listed in Chapter 8 of *WTW*; and you may find it interesting and helpful to check a word's origin in several different places. You might want to share the picture book by E. H. Fine, *Cryptomania: Teleporting into Greek and Latin with the Cryptokids*. The cryptokids travel to different places and times to see how widespread these roots really are. Ideally you will create a classroom environment where students are curious about word origins and will want to investigate any interesting word that turns up.

Students should be encouraged to return to prefixes and suffixes studied in earlier units and use those to add to the words in the sorts; for example, *respect* can become *respective, respected, respectful, respectfully, disrespectful*. Have them work cooperatively to create word trees and word webs (described in Chapter 8) and record these in their word study notebook. Also encourage them to play with Greek and Latin elements to create their own original words. *Photoscope* might not be a real word but it could be. New products and new ideas require new terminology (i.e., *photocopier, instamatic, camcorder*) and Greek and Latin elements continue to be drawn upon to coin these words.

Jeopardy is a favorite game that lends itself to the review of Latin and Greek roots and there is a good example in Chapter 8 of *WTW*. Quartet, Brainburst, Rootwebs, and other games and activities can be found there as well. Many games described in Chapter 6 can be adapted by substituting roots for vowel patterns. Vowel Poker becomes Root Poker by creating sets of cards featuring words in the same meaning family: *rupture, corrupt, erupt, disrupt, interrupt*.

Cognates are common in the higher level academic vocabulary studied in these sorts because all romance languages such as Spanish, French, and Italian have thousands of words derived from Greek and Latin as does English. Attention to these cognates will help ELLs learn English more readily and will help native English speakers who may be studying a foreign language. Cognates can sometimes be found by looking through language dictionaries. For example, if you look up words starting with *frac-* in an *English-Spanish* dictionary, you will find *fracción* (fraction), *fraccionario* ("to break up"), and *fractura* (fracture).

SORT 25   GREEK AND LATIN NUMBER PREFIXES (*MONO-, UNI-, BI-, TRI-*)

(See page 83.) This sort introduces the Greek prefix *mono-* which means "one" and reviews three Latin prefixes taught in the late syllables and affixes stage: *uni-* which also means "one," *bi-* which means "two," and *tri-* which means "three." Spanish has these same prefixes: *monotony = monotonia, uniform = uniforme, tricycle = tricliclo, bicycle = bicicleta*. (Note, however, that *mono* means "monkey" in Spanish.)

Demonstrate, Sort, and Reflect

Prepare a set of words to use for teacher-directed modeling. Save the discussion of word meanings until after sorting. Display a transparency of the words on the overhead or hand out the sheet of words to the students. Ask them what they notice about the words and get ideas about how the words can be sorted. Students usually notice that all the words contain prefixes. Remind them of the term **prefixes** (units added to the beginning of a word). Put up the headers and sort the rest of the words. Begin the reflection by discussing the meanings of the words they recognize and arrive at some conclusions about what each prefix means. In this context, ask them to discuss the difference between *monolingual* and *bilingual*, explicitly referring to what *lingual* means ("language"). This discussion will help establish how these words may be analyzed according to prefix and the remaining meaning element. Students will then have activated their prior knowledge about these prefixes enough to support analyzing the less-familiar words. Dictionaries should be used to look up the meaning of words that are less transparent, such as *biennial.*

You may mention a number of roots, combining forms, and their meanings in the context of this sort. For example, have students heard the word *triathlon? triathlete?* Do they see a similarity between *triathlon* and *athletic?* Where have they heard *trilogy?* (Most students will probably mention *Lord of the Rings*; others may mention *Star Wars* or other science fiction trilogies.) If someone speaks in a *monotone*, would it be interesting and exciting to listen to him? Similarly, if you speak about the *monotony* of a situation or experience, would that situation or experience be exciting? Since *bi-* means "two" and *sect* comes from *section*, what does it mean to say that an interstate highway *bisects* a city?

mono-	uni-	bi-	tri-
monolingual	**uniform**	**bilingual**	**triangle**
monologue	universal	biceps	triad
monotonous	unilateral	bisect	triceratops
monopoly	unify	binary	trilogy
monorail		bimonthly	triathlon
monotone		bifocals	tripod
		biennial	trillion

Extend

As a point of interest, tell students that in English we also have, of course, the word *two*: Have they thought about the relationship between *two*, *twin*, and *twice*? How about *three* and *thrice*? The number *three* is significant in mythology and religion. Have students be on the lookout for significant occurrences of *three*.

Additional Words. *monarch, monochrome, monocle, monogamist, monolith, monopolize, monopod, unification, unisex, unity, unitarian, university, universe, bicameral, bicentennial, bicuspid, bifurcate, bigamist, bilateral, binoculars, bipartisan, bipolar, bisexual, biped, biplane, biweekly, tricolor, trident, trilobite, trimester, triple, triplicate, triennial, trigonometry, trillium, trivet, triptych, trisect, trinity, triumvirate*

SORT 26   MORE NUMBER PREFIXES

(See page 84.) This sort introduces number prefixes: *quadr-* and *quar-*, which both mean "four"; *quint-* and *pent-*, which both mean "five"; *-oct* which means "eight," *dec-*, which means "ten," and *cent-* which means "one hundred."

Demonstrate

Have students sort the words according to number prefix. Have them discuss any words they know or at least have seen or heard. Speculate as to their meaning. Although students may know that *quintuplets* refers to five siblings born at the same time, share with them that the word *quintessence*, which refers to the purest or highest essence of something—"She was the *quintessence* of gymnastic ability"—historically and literally means the fifth and highest "essence" after the essences of air, earth, fire, and water. The sentence, "We now have the *quintessential* recipe for tacos" means that the recipe is the most representative one for tacos. *Decimate* originally referred to the killing of every tenth person, a punishment used in the Roman army for mutinous legions. Today this means the killing of any large proportion of a group.

Now that several number prefixes have been explored, share with the students *why* there are different prefixes for "one," "two," "four," "five," and so forth: Greek had its own words for these elements, Latin had other words. Both sets of number elements survived and continued to be passed down through other languages without significant change.

quadr-/quar-	quint-/pent-	oct-	dec-	cent-
quartet	quintet	octet	decimal	centimeter
quarter	quintuplets	octagon	decathlon	century
quadrangle	quintessence	octave	decade	centigrade
quadruped	quintessential		decimate	centennial
quadruple	pentagon			bicentennial
quadruplets				percentage

Extend

Have students collect other words they come across that contain number prefixes and write them in their vocabulary notebooks. If the meaning of a word is not obvious, they should write the sentence in which it occurs as well. Other number prefixes include *di/du* (2) as in *duet* and *dioxide*, *tetra* (4) as in *tetrahedron*, *sex/hex* (6) as in *sextent* and *hexagon*, *hept/sept* (7) as in *heptagon* and *September*, *non/nov* (9) as in *November* and *nonagon*, and *milli/kilo* (one thousand) as in *million* and *kilometer*.

Additional Words.   *quandrant, quart, quadrennial, quartile, pentameter, pentathion, octagonal, octopus, octane, October, octogenarian, quintuple, quintillion, decagon, December, decibel, decimeter, centipede, percent*

SORT 27   GREEK AND LATIN ELEMENTS: SIZE (*MICRO-*, *MEGA-*, *SUPER-*, *HYPER-*)

(See page 85.) This sort focuses on Greek combining forms: *micro-*, which means "small"; *mega-*, which means "great"; *hyper-*, which means "over" or "beyond"; and the inclusion of one Latin form: *super-*, which also means "over" or "above." Introduce the sort by telling the students that a large number of words contain these elements, three of which come from Greek and one from Latin.

Demonstrate, Sort, and Reflect

Have the students sort the words by the elements *micro-*, *mega-*, *super-*, and *hyper-*. After they have completed the sort, have them discuss the *micro* words. Most students already have an idea, of course, about the meaning of *micro-*, but it is important for them to think explicitly about the way in which it combines. You may say: "*Microscope* is literally looking at or targeting something very small." For the word *microcosm*, share the following quote from the Russian developmental psychologist Lev Vygotsky: "A word is a *microcosm* of human experience." Students will realize that this refers to a small part of experience; ask them if they can think of any other words that have *cosm* in them. Share that *cosm* comes from the Greek form *cosmo-*, meaning "order, world/universe." The ancient Greeks conceived of the world or universe as a well-ordered entity. Therefore, the word *cosmos* refers to a well-ordered universe, and *cosmopolitan* refers to something of "worldly" importance. Then, go back to *microcosm*: A word is a "small world" of human experience—not just a "small part"—because each word represents so much of human experience. *Microbe* is a combination of *micro* and *biology*, literally, "small form of life."

The meanings of *super-* and *hyper-* are similar. Most of the words in this sort lend themselves to a straightforward presentation, but students should still analyze each word and reflect on how the prefix and base word combine to result in the meaning of the word.

micro-	mega-	super-	hyper-
microwave	**megaphone**	**supermarket**	**hyperactive**
microcosm	megalopolis	superhero	hyperventilate
microscope	megabyte	superhighway	hyperbole
microbus	megadose	superhuman	hypercritical
microfilm	megahit	superstar	hypersensitive
microsurgery		superego	
microbe		superpower	

Extend

Contrast *hyper-* with *hypo-*, which means *under, below,* or *beneath*. Students may be familiar with *hypothermia* (lowered temperature) or *hypodermic* (under the skin). Also contrast *micro* with *macro*, which means "large or inclusive," in words such as *macrocosm* (the whole world) and *macroscopic* (large enough to be seen without a microscope).

Have students generate other words that include *micro-*, *mega-*, *super-*, and *hyper-*. Some may be actual words, others may not. For each word generated, they should write a brief definition and/or sentence that includes the word appropriately.

Additional Words. *microcomputer, microchip, micrometer, microorganism, Micronesia, microphone, megalomaniac, megaton, megavitamins, megawatt, supercharge, supercilious, supercomputer, superconductor, superficial, supervise, supervision, superintendent, superior, superlative, supernatural, superstar, superstition, supersonic, supertanker, hyperglycemic, hypertension, hypertext, hyperthyroidism*

SORT 28 GREEK ROOTS (*TELE*, *PHON*, *PHOTO*, *GRAPH*)

(See page 86.) This sort offers robust opportunities for exploring Greek elements and how they work: *tele-*, which means "distant"; *phon-*, which means "sound"; *photo-*, which means "light"; and *graph-*, which means "write." When these elements combine with other Greek elements, the resulting meaning is usually obvious or transparent. Students should think directly about the meaning of each of these elements and examine, discuss, and understand how the meanings of these word parts combine to result in the meaning of a word.

Demonstrate, Sort, and Reflect

Introduce this sort by telling the students that many words contain these Greek roots and that these roots usually have a pretty consistent meaning. They usually do not occur by themselves as words, although sometimes they do. Tell the students that learning the meanings of these roots and understanding how they combine to create words will be extremely helpful in figuring out and learning new vocabulary through their reading as well as in correcting occasional spelling errors.

Have the students sort all the *tele-* words and read through the words in the list. Ask students what they think *tele* might mean in these words. Then tell them that *tele* comes from Greek and means "distant." Ask students if they see a smaller word within *television* (*vision*). When *tele* combines with *vision*, it literally means "vision from a distance." Discuss why this is, literally, what *television* is and does—it delivers vision from a distance (by cable, satellite, or antenna).

Next sort words with *phon* (this will include *telephone* from the previous sort). Read through the words and ask students what *phon* seems to mean. Discuss that *phone* in *telephone* comes from a Greek word that means "sound." When it combines with *tele*, it literally means "sound from a distance." *Microphone* (note the prefix from the last sort) literally means "small sound," so discuss how a microphone is not *literally* a small sound but that it is a device that picks up sounds that otherwise would not be heard very well.

Repeat the sorting with *photo* and *graph* and read through the words to establish that *photo* means "light" and *graph* means "to write or record something." Elicit definitions and explanations from the students, though you may need to scaffold their explanations for particular words. Students have probably heard about the *telegraph*, but perhaps not thought about the fact that it means, literally, "writing from a distance." You may need to scaffold discussion of *telephoto*; the students have probably heard the word in the context of a telephoto lens but not reflected on the meaning. This often leads to a productive discussion about the literal meaning of *telephoto*—"light from a distance." Discuss *photography*—literally "writing with light"—because there is usually at least one student who understands the process by which photography works. If not, this may be a good time to mention the process briefly; for example, the lens lets in light that is "written" onto film or a disk (as with a digital camera).

This may be a good time to mention how the prefix *sym-/syn-* works. Meaning "together, with," *sym-/syn-* occurs with considerable frequency, and also comes from Greek. Tell students that *synthesis* means "combining or bringing together separate pieces to form a whole." The word *photosynthesis*, therefore, literally means "bringing together" or "synthesizing" light. Share with the students that they don't have to go into the details of photosynthesis, which probably are understandable only to biologists. They need only to understand that photosynthesis is an important process that plants utilize to stay alive and grow.

tele	*phon*	*photo*	*graph*
television	**phonics**	**photograph***	**graphic**
telecast	phonograph*	photocopier	graphite
telegraph*	headphone	photosynthesis	paragraph
telegram	homophone	photographer	autograph
telephoto*	microphone	photogenic	choreography
telephone*	xylophone	telephoto*	calligraphy
	symphony	phonograph*	telegraph*
	telephone*		photograph*

*These words will be sorted in more than one category.

Extend

This is a good time to begin a chart of roots that you will continue to add to across many lessons to come. Students can also establish a section of their vocabulary notebooks to list these as well.

Additional Words. *telethon, telecommunications, teleconference, telepathy, cacophony, euphony, saxophone, photoelectric, photons, digraph, topography, bibliography, videographer, ethnography, seismograph*

SORT 29   MORE GREEK ROOTS (*GEO, THERM, SCOPE, METER, LOGY*)

(See page 87.) More Greek roots are introduced in this sort: *geo-*, which means "earth"; *therm*, which means "heat"; *scope*, which means "target or see"; *meter-*, which means "measure"; and *logy*, which means "study."

Sort and Reflect

Conduct this sort in a manner similar to the one above. Have students discuss the unfamiliar terms, debating what the meaning might be, based on their inference from the combination of the word parts. Discussion of how the meanings of the Greek forms combine to result in the meaning of each word is critical. *Peri* is a useful element to add to the discussions. It means "around" so that *periscope* would mean "to look around" and *perimeter* would mean "to measure around." Talk briefly about the meaning of the number prefixes *milli* (thousand) and *kilo* (hundred). *Geometry* also has the root *geo* but is less obviously connected with the earth; however, geometry was orginally developed by the Greeks to measure land. Be sure to talk about *etymology*—the study of word orgins!

geo	therm	scope	meter	logy
geography	**thermal**	**telescope**	**perimeter**	**mythology**
geology*	thermometer*	periscope	barometer	ecology
geothermal*	thermostat	stethoscope	millimeter	zoology
geode	thermos	microscope	kilometer	etymology
geometry	geothermal*	horoscope	diameter	geology*
			speedometer	
			thermometer*	

*These words should be sorted in more than one category.

Extend

A spelling convention began in Roman times in which a "connecting vowel" was often inserted between two word parts: If one word part ends with a consonant and the next word part begins with a consonant, a vowel—usually *o* or *i*—is inserted; for example, *thermometer, mythology.*

"Combining Roots and Affixes," described in Chapter 8, in *WTW* is an excellent follow-up activity to this sort, as well as to later sorts in which Greek and Latin elements are explored.

Additional Words. *geophysics, geocentric, thermonuclear, thermodynamic, exothermic, gyroscope, kaleidoscope, tachometer, altimeter, pathology, psychology, sociology, theology, genealogy, technology*

SORT 30 LATIN ROOTS (*SPECT, PORT, FORM*)

(See page 88.) This sort explores the Latin roots *spect,* which means "to look at"; *port,* which means "to carry"; and *form,* which means to "shape." The meanings of these Latin roots are straightforward, as are the meanings of most of the words in which they combine with other affixes and roots. As with the Greek roots or combining forms in Sorts 28 and 29, these Latin roots occur frequently in printed materials from the intermediate grades onward. In this sort many prefixes will be reviewed from earlier sorts.

Demonstrate, Sort, and Reflect

Because this sort is the first of many that will explore Latin word roots, you may wish to begin by walking the students through two or three words, explaining how the elements combine to produce the meaning of the word. (The teacher scripts in Chapter 8 of *WTW* are good models for this type of explanation.)

Begin by writing the word *inspection* on the board or the overhead. Ask the students to explain the meaning of *inspection,* and use the word in a sentence. Then tell them that the word is made up of the suffix *-ion* (the "act or result" of something), the Latin root *-spec-,* which means "to look at," and the prefix *in-,* meaning "into." Now have the students think about it: Given their explanation and definition of *inspection,* do they see that the combination of these word parts literally means "the act of looking into" something?

Have students sort the words according to the root in each. Follow up by having students discuss, in pairs, how they think the word parts combine to produce the meaning of each word. Contrast *export* (carry out) and *import* (carry in). *Important* will be hard to reconcile with other *port* words since it literally means "carried in." Metaphorically it might mean "carrying weight." Following are other words that you may walk through with the students after they sort and discuss them: *perspective*, "look through" (when you talk about your *perspective* on an issue or on life you are actually talking about how you have *looked through* that issue); *prospect*, "look forward." Point out to the students that, for the vast majority of words that appear to contain a word root, they can best analyze the words by beginning at the end of the word: Reflect on how you analyzed the word *inspection*.

spect	port	form
inspection	**export**	**conform**
perspective	portable	deformed
retrospect	import	format
spectator	transport	formation
inspector	reporter	reform
prospect	portfolio	transform
aspect	important	
spectacle	support	
spectacular		
prospector		

Extend

Take time to discuss the prefix *trans-* meaning "across" and brainstorm other words that start with it: *transfer, transplant, transmit, transcontinental*. Add it to your prefix chart.

Several words offer possibilities for generating additional words derived from them by adding *-ion* or *-ation*. Have students see how many derived words they can generate, first by discussing whether the derived words really exist or not, and then checking the dictionary to confirm or not; for example, *transportation, transformation, reformation*. Review with students the idea that words are changed from verbs to nouns with the addition of *-tion*. Also note the vowel alternation from *format* to *formation*.

Additional Words. *expect, expectation, introspective, retrospective, spectacles, spectrum, specimen, suspect, airport, seaport, comportment, deport, heliport, importune, opportune, portage, portmanteau, rapport, deformity, formal, formula, informal, information, malformed, platform, uniform*

SORT 31 LATIN ROOTS (*DIC, AUD, VIS*)

(See page 89.) This sort explores the Latin roots *dic*, which means "to say or speak"; *aud*, which means "to hear"; and *vis*, which means "to see." As with Sort 30, the meanings of these Latin roots are straightforward, as are the meanings of most of the words in which they combine with other affixes and roots.

Demonstrate, Sort, and Reflect

Begin by writing the words *dictate, audible,* and *vision* on the board or the overhead. Ask the students to explain the meaning of *dictate* and use the word in a sentence. Continue this introduction with the words *audible* and *vision*. Depending on the students' response, encourage them to speculate about the meanings of the roots. Sort the words and discuss the meanings of other words to help the students arrive at some conclusions about the meanings of the roots. *Laudable* is an "oddball"; it means "praiseworthy" and does not contain the root *aud*.

Following are other words that you may walk through with the students after they sort and discuss them: *unpredictable*—after *un-* and *-able* are removed, the base word *predict* remains. Literally, *predict* means "to say before"; put *-able* back on and discuss what *predictable* means, then put *un-* back on and discuss what *unpredictable* means. Take *supervisor* apart in a similar way. *Supervise* means to "see over" or "look over from above" and the *-or* suffix indicates "one who does this." *Contra-* is not a common prefix but it means "against" and shows up in both *contraband* and *contrary*. *Dictionaries* do not "speak" but are full of the words that make up our speech.

dic	*aud*	*vis*	oddball
dictate	**audible**	**vision**	laudable
contradict	auditorium	visible	
unpredictable	audition	supervisor	
dictator	audience	vista	
edict	audiotape	visitor	
dictionary	auditory	invisible	
prediction	audiovisual	revisit	
		(audiovisual)	

Additional Words.   *abdicate, diction, dictum, dedicate, indict, jurisdiction, valedictorian, vindicate, verdict, inaudible, audiology, visage, visit, visa, visual, advise, envision, provision, improvise*

SORT 32   LATIN ROOTS (*GRESS*, *RUPT*, *TRACT*, *MOT*)

(See page 90.) This sort covers the Latin roots *gress*, which means "to go"; *rupt*, which means "to break"; *tract*, which means "to draw or pull"; and *mot*, which means "to move." As with the roots in the previous two sorts, these roots occur with considerable frequency.

Background Information

Draw on students' knowledge of prefixes as you discuss the words.

Progress = gress "to go" + *pro* "forward"—so *progress* literally means "to move forward."

Interrupt = rupt "to break" + *inter* "between"—so *interrupt* literally means "to break in between," which is what you do when you *interrupt* a conversation.

Detract = tract "to draw or pull" + *de* "away, apart"—so *detract* literally means "to draw away from," which is what happens when something *detracts* from what you want people to pay attention to. ("Your hollering about why you like your candidate *detracts* from your goal of getting people to vote for her.")

Promote = mot(e) "to move" + *pro* "forward"—so when you *promote* an idea, you move that idea forward.

Sort and Reflect

Have the students sort the words according to the root. As in the previous sort, have students pair up to discuss the meanings of each of the words. Then regroup to discuss any of the words about which they were uncertain. The use of a dictionary with etymological information will come in handy here. Tell the students that they may notice these elements in other words, but that you will be exploring the elements in depth later on. For example, *attract* and *aggressive* actually contain the absorbed prefix *ad-*, meaning "to or toward"; this and other absorbed prefixes are addressed in Sorts 56 to 59. In several of the words *e-* is a prefix meaning "out"; for example, when a volcano *erupts* it literally "breaks out"; *emotion* literally means "the act or result of moving out"—discuss with students how this word has come to possess the connotative meaning it has now. When someone is *emotional*, what "moves out" from within them? Point out that the base word of *emotion* is *emote*, a word that we don't run across nearly as often as *emotion*. Where do they think the word *emoticon* comes from? What word is combined with *emotion/emote* to create *emoticon*? (*icon*) (:

gress	rupt	tract	mot
progress	**interrupt**	**detract**	**promote**
regress	erupt	distract	motion
digress	rupture	traction	demote
aggressive	abrupt	attract	locomotive
egress	disrupt	extract	motivate
transgress		tractor	emotion
			emoticon

Extend

Ask students to look for words that they can change to or add the *-ion* ending: *progression, regression, aggression, interruption, attraction, locomotion*.

Additional Words. *congress, ingress, bankrupt, corrupt, contract, retract, protracted, intractable, abstract, emote, motor, remote, automobile, motivation, motel, locomotion, commotion*

SORT 33   LATIN ROOTS (*FRACT, FLECT/FLEX, JECT, MIS/MIT*)

(See page 91.) This sort covers the Latin roots *fract*, meaning "to break"; *flect* or *flex*, meaning "to bend"; *ject*, meaning "to throw"; and *mis* or *mit*, meaning "to send."

Sort and Reflect

Have the students sort the words according to the root. Have them sort individually, and then have them compare their sorts with those of a partner to see if they had different categories. Some students will sort according to the spelling of the root so that words containing *flex* and *flect*, for example, will be in different groups. Have the students then discuss what they think each root means. Guide their discussion by focusing first on the more obvious or literally apparent combinations: for example, *fraction* is "the result of breaking" something into smaller pieces; *reject* is to "throw back." You may facilitate discussion of some of the more semantically opaque combinations, such as *objection*. An *objection* is, literally, "the act or result of throwing against" (*ob* means "against"). More connotatively, making an *objection* is "throwing" a verbal point against someone. Mention *permission*: Which word does it come from? How about *transmission*? Mention also that *trajectory* actually comes from the combination of the prefix *trans-* "across" + *-ject-*, literally "to throw across"; "the long *trajectory* of the soccer ball as it soared over the heads of the other team." *Fractious* actually comes from an old sense of *fraction*, which meant "discord." If you use the word *fractious* to refer to someone's behavior, how might you characterize or describe that behavior?

fract	flect/flex	ject	mis/mit
fracture	**reflect**	**reject**	**transmit**
fraction	flexible	eject	emissions
infraction	deflect	projector	admit
fractious	reflex	injection	permit
	inflexible	project*	mission
	reflector	trajectory	submit
		object*	submission

*Homographs can be stressed on either syllable: *project* or *project*, *object* or *object*.

Extend

What other words can the students create with other affixes (e.g., *inflexible* or *flexiblity*)? Review the suffix and spelling changes when the suffix is added in *projection, rejection, deflection, reflection, emission, permission*, and so forth.

Pull out the words *submit* and *submission*. Talk about the spelling change when -*ion* is added (the *t* changes to *ss*). Then write up the words *transmit, emit, admit, remit*, and *permit* and ask students to pronounce and spell the derived form with -*ion*. Changing from *mit* to *miss* when adding *ion* is an example of an unusual but predictable change that can be added to your chart of generalizations governing the addition of -*ion*.

Additional Words. *fractals, projectile, refract, refraction, flex, reflection, reflective, inflect, circumflex, genuflect, interject, conjecture, abject, dejected, subjective, commit, commision, emit, emissary, intermission, intermittent, missile, missionary, omit, omission, permission, remit, remission*

SORT 34   LATIN ROOTS (MAN, *SCRIB*/*SCRIPT*, *CRED*, *FAC*)

(See page 92.) This sort explores the Latin roots *man*, meaning "hand"; *scrib/script*, meaning "to write"; *cred*, meaning "to believe"; and *fac*, meaning "to make."

Background Information

Man and *scrib/script* are usually straightforward—*manual* labor is working by hand, *manuscript* is writing by hand. Students will probably be quite curious about *manure*, however! Share with them that, etymologically, *manure* is actually closely related to *manual*: *Manure* evolved from a Middle English word that meant "to cultivate land," which in turn evolved from a Latin word that meant "to work with the hands." Ask the students how they think people hundreds of years ago actually cultivated their land, knowing what they know about the present-day meaning of *manure*.

Contrast *credible* and *incredible*. Since *incredible* is the more common word discuss its meaning, first, then ask students what they think *credible* means. Scaffold their understanding that if something is *incredible*, it is literally "not believable." *Credence* may also be unfamiliar: "Because she is so knowledgeable about setting up a website, I put a lot of *credence* in her advice."

The way the root *fac* works in *factory* and *manufacture* is straightforward. Ask students if they see a familiar pattern in *facsimile*. After *fac* is removed, *simile* remains. What do they think *simile* might mean? For most students, this is the first time they become aware that "similar" is in *facsimile*—literally, "make similar." Isn't that what a *fax* machine does? (This may also be the first time that students realize *fax* is short for *facsimile*.) *Artifact* is a good example of a word whose literal sum of its meaning parts—"something made from art"—no longer exactly fits, but allows you to discuss a more connotative meaning: something made by humans at a different time and in a different culture.

Demonstrate, Sort, and Reflect

On the first day, work with the words as you did in earlier sorts. Students may sort these words without teacher introduction. Have them first sort individually, then compare with a partner. Students will notice that *manufacture* and *manuscript* may be sorted in more than one category. Ask them to discuss with their partners what they think each root might mean. After partner discussions, discuss the meanings that the students have generated. Address roots about which the students are uncertain. After discussing some of the *scrib/script* words, ask students where the word *scribble* came from—most students will not have consciously made this connection.

On the second day of working with these words, you may elect to discuss why the spelling of some roots changes across related words (e.g., *scrib/script; fac/fic/fect*). These forms come from the original Latin verbs, in which the sound changed in different forms, and therefore the spelling changed as well. This happens in many English verbs too: *do, did, done, was, were*, etc.

man	scrib/script	cred	fac
manual	**transcribe**	**incredible**	**factory**
manuscript*	prescribe	credible	artifact
manicure	prescription	credence	facsimile
manure	inscribe	discredit	facilitate
mandate	inscription	incredulous	manufacture*
maneuver	scribe		
manufacture*	subscription		
	scribble		
	manuscript*		

*These words can be sorted in two categories.

Extend

Pull out the words *prescribe, prescription, inscribe,* and *inscription*. Talk about the spelling change to the root before adding *-ion*. Ask students to generate other *scrib/script* words ending in *-ion* (e.g., *subscribe/subscription, describe/description, transcribe/transcription*). Like *mit* to *miss* above, this is another unusual, but predictable, spelling change when adding *-ion* to words with the root *scribe*.

By this point, students have explored a sufficient number of Latin and Greek elements to play Greek and Latin Jeopardy (see Chapter 8 of *WTW*). This is an extremely popular game format with students and is one that will continue to grow with the students' advancing word knowledge. Eventually students can prepare their own Jeopardy games, exploring new roots as well as using the format to develop and reinforce content-area vocabulary in science, math, and social studies, for example. Other Greek- and Latin-element games in Chapter 8 of *WTW* may also be explored here and in subsequent units.

Additional Words. *emancipate, manacle, manipulate, manage, ascribe, circumscribe, conscription, describe, postscript, scripture, script, scriptwriter, subscribe, credit, credentials, incredible, accredited, credulous, faculty, benefactor, facile*

ASSESSMENT 5 FOR SORTS 25–34

Use the form on page 93 to assess students' knowledge of root meanings. Ask them to write the letter of the correct match. Below is the answer key.

1. cred (f)	a. three		1. flect (c)	a. hundred
2. mono (c)	b. carry		2. aud (f)	b. heat
3. bi (i)	c. one		3. form (e)	c. bend
4. spect (g)	d. speak		4. geo (i)	d. sound
5. port (b)	e. hand		5. cent (a)	e. shape
6. fac (j)	f. believe		6. gress (h)	f. hear
7. dic (d)	g. see		7. tele (j)	g. break
8. man (e)	h. throw		8. rupt (g)	h. go
9. tri (a)	i. two		9. therm (b)	i. earth
10. ject (h)	j. do		10. phon (d)	j. far

Ask students to spell and define the following words:

1. monotony	2. trilogy	3. microsurgery	4. hypercritical
5. emissions	6. geothermal	7. quadruped	8. bicentennial
9. retrospect	10. opportune	11. periscope	12. audience
13. contradict	14. aggressive	15. interrupt	16. distract
17. trajectory	18. incredulous	19. facsimile	20. spectacle

SORT 25   Greek and Latin Number Prefixes (*mono-*, *uni-*, *bi-*, *tri-*)

mono-	*uni-*	*bi-*	*tri-*

uniform	**monolingual**	**bilingual**
triangle	monologue	tripod
biceps	unilateral	triad
trilogy	monotonous	unify
bifocals	triceratops	bisect
monorail	bimonthly	monopoly
binary	universal	triathlon
biennial	monotone	trillion

SORT 26   More Number Prefixes

quadr- quar-	quint- pent-	oct-	dec-	cent-
quartet	**quintet**		**octet**	
decimal	**centimeter**		pentagon	
octagon	quadrangle		century	
quadruped	quintuplets		quarter	
decathlon	centigrade		octave	
centennial	quintessence		quadruple	
decade	quadruplets		decimate	
bicentennial	quintessential		percentage	

SORT 27   Greek and Latin Elements: Size (*micro-*, *mega-*, *super-*, *hyper-*)

micro-	*mega-*	*super-*	*hyper-*
microwave	**megaphone**	**supermarket**	
hyperactive	microcosm	megalopolis	
superhero	hyperventilate	microscope	
megabyte	superhighway	hyperbole	
microbus	hypercritical	megadose	
superstar	microsurgery	superego	
microbe	hypersensitive	superhuman	
megahit	superpower	microfilm	

SORT 28   Greek Roots (*tele*, *phon*, *photo*, *graph*)

tele	*phon*	*photo*	*graph*
television		**phonics**	**photograph**
graphic		telecast	autograph
photocopier		graphite	headphone
telegraph		photosynthesis	paragraph
homophone		photographer	telegram
phonograph		telephoto	microphone
photogenic		choreography	telephone
xylophone		calligraphy	symphony

SORT 29   More Greek Roots (*geo, therm, scope, meter, logy*)

geo	therm	scope	meter	logy

geography	thermal	telescope
perimeter	mythology	geology
periscope	thermometer	barometer
geothermal	microscope	horoscope
thermostat	speedometer	millimeter
ecology	stethoscope	geode
thermos	etymology	kilometer
zoology	diameter	geometry

SORT 30   Latin Roots (*spect, port, form*)

spect	*port*	*form*
inspection	**export**	**conform**
deformed	perspective	portable
retrospect	import	format
formation	spectator	transport
inspector	reporter	reform
transform	prospect	important
spectacle	spectacular	support
aspect	prospector	portfolio

SORT 31   Latin Roots (*dic, aud, vis*)

dic	*aud*	*vis*
dictate	**audible**	**vision**
visible	contradict	audition
vista	auditorium	invisible
revisit	unpredictable	prediction
dictionary	supervisor	dictator
edict	audiovisual	auditory
laudable	audiotape	audience
visitor	laudable	

SORT 32   Latin Roots (*gress, rupt, tract, mot*)

gress	*rupt*	*tract*	*mot*
progress		**interrupt**	**detract**
promote		regress	erupt
distract		motion	digress
rupture		traction	demote
aggressive		abrupt	attract
egress		locomotive	disrupt
extract		transgress	motivate
tractor		emotion	emoticon

SORT 33   Latin Roots (*fract, flect/flex, ject, mis/mit*)

fract	*flect/flex*	*ject*	*mis/mit*
fracture		**reflect**	**reject**
transmit		fraction	flexible
eject		emissions	infraction
deflect		projector	admit
fractious		inflexible	reflex
injection		submission	permit
mission		reflector	submit
object		trajectory	project

SORT 34 Latin Roots (*man*, *scrib/script*, *cred*, *fac*)

man	*scrib/script*	*cred*	*fac*
manual	**transcribe**		**incredible**
factory	manuscript		prescribe
credible	manufacture		manicure
credence	prescription		facsimile
manure	inscribe		discredit
facilitate	inscription		mandate
artifact	subscription		maneuver
scribble	incredulous		scribe

ASSESSMENT 5 FOR SORTS 25–34
Beside each root write the letter of the matching meaning.

Name _____

a. hundred	1. flect
b. heat	2. aud
c. bend	3. form
d. sound	4. geo
e. shape	5. cent
f. hear	6. gress
g. break	7. tele
h. go	8. rupt
i. earth	9. therm
j. far	10. phon

a. three	1. cred
b. carry	2. mono
c. one	3. bi
d. speak	4. spect
e. hand	5. port
f. believe	6. fac
g. see	7. dic
h. throw	8. man
i. two	9. tri
j. do	10. ject

Unit VI Greek and Latin Elements II

NOTES FOR THE TEACHER

See the teacher notes on page 69 (Greek and Latin Elements I) which still apply here. In addition to some common, straightforward roots, many of the elements explored in this section are elements that have evolved from their literal meaning to a more connotative meaning. They are studied because they occur across a wide range of content areas and domains. In addition, several of the roots are grouped topically, such as those related to the *body*.

SORT 35 LATIN ROOTS (*DUC/DUCT, SEQU/SEC, FLU, VER/VERT*)

(See page 105.) This sort explores the roots *duc* or *duct* meaning "lead," *sequ* or *sec* meaning "follow," *flu* meaning "flow," and *ver* or *vert* meaning "turn."

Demonstrate, Sort, and Reflect

Prepare a set of words to use for teacher-directed modeling. Save the discussion of word meanings until after sorting. Display a transparency of the words on the overhead or hand out the sheet of words to the students. Ask them what they notice about the words and get ideas about how the words can be sorted. Students usually notice that the words can be sorted by roots. Students will want to sort words with *sequ* separate from *sec* but will see after discussing the meaning of the words that they can go together.

   After sorting, ask students to read through the words in each column to generate a hypothesis about what the roots might mean. Have students discuss the literal meanings of *introduce* ("to lead in") and *introduction* ("the act or result of leading in"). Do they see how the meaning of each word has connotatively evolved into its present meaning? In the words *affluence* and *superfluous*, the root *flu* takes on a more metaphorical sense of "abundance" or "plenty" as in wealth flows to those who have affluence. The root *ver* or *vert* literally means "turn back" in *reverse*. *Convert* and *conversation* have rather different meanings but talk about how each involves turning.

duc/duct	sequ/sec	flu	ver/vert
introduction	**sequel**	**fluid**	**reverse**
induce	consequence	fluent	inverse
conductor	subsequent	influx	convert
abduct	sect	affluence	vertigo
reduce	consecutive	fluctuate	conversation
educate		superfluous	extravert
deduct			

Extend

Have the students identify the base word and derived words *invert/inversion*, *deduct/deduction*, and so forth. Note that *conversion* is derived from *convert* whereas *conversation* is derived from *converse*. This sort affords you the opportunity to discuss why the spelling of the root changes: The phonology or pronunciation exerts an influence. For example, when the noun *conversion* was formed from the verb *convert* it was easier to say "conver*zh*un" than "conver*sh*un," and so the spelling had to reflect this pronunciation. Note, however, that *most* of the time the root's spelling *does* remain the same: *ver*.

Write *introduce* and *introduction* on the board. Use both in a sentence to review their parts of speech: When you *introduce* (verb) someone you make an *introduction* (noun). Talk about the vowel sound that alternates (long *u* to short *u*) and the consonant sound that alternates (soft *c* to hard *c*). Discuss how, in addition to dropping the *e* in the *-uce* words, a *t* must be added to *-ion*. If the students want to pursue the reason for this, you might ask them how the suffixed word would be spelled if the *t* were not added (e.g., *producion*). How might it be pronounced? (Perhaps something like "proDOOshun.") Share with the students that English has evolved such that there's no such spelling or pronunciation. The *t* was added to *-ion* to keep the hard sound of the *c*. Write up *educate* and *education*. Do any sounds alternate in this pair? No, the vowels stay long in both, but the *e* is dropped before adding *-ion*. Add this to your list of predictable spelling changes when adding *-ion*. Provide a list of words and ask students to write and pronounce the derived form with *-tion*: *abduct, deduce, induce, reduce, conduct, produce, reproduce, seduce*.

Note that the word *conduct* is a homograph whose meaning and part of speech depends upon the accented syllable. If you *conduct* yourself properly you may be rewarded for your *conduct*. Can you and your students spot any other homographs among the words? *Convert* can also be both a verb and a noun depending on the accent.

Additonal Words. *aqueduct, abduction, deduce, deduction, duct, conduct, educe, induct, produce, reproduce, seduce, viaduct, seque, non sequitor, persecute, confluence, effluent, effluvium, flue, fluency, flume, flush, influence, mellifluous, superfluity, averse, aversion, advertise, conversion, controversy, divert, diverse, diversion, invert, introvert, pervert, perversion, subvert, subversive, transverse, universe, verastile, versus, vertex, version, vertebra*

SORT 36   LATIN ROOTS (*BENE, MAL*) AND PREFIXES (*ANTE-, POST-*)

(See page 106.) This sort addresses the Latin roots *bene*, meaning "good or well"; *mal*, meaning "bad"; and prefixes *ante-*, meaning "before"; and *post-*, meaning "after."

Background Information

Dismal = "bad day." *Dis* is not a prefix, but rather comes from the Latin *dies*, which means "day." So, *dismal* literally means "bad day."

Malaria = "bad air." Originally the cause of malaria was literally thought to be "bad air."

Maladroit = "not adroit." Ask the students what the base word of *maladroit* is—have they heard of it? If someone is *adroit* at something, what does that mean? So, if someone is *maladroit*, what does that mean?

Demonstrate, Sort, and Reflect

This sort contrasts two word roots, *bene* and *mal*, and two prefixes, *ante-* and *post*. The emphasis here is on their combination with other roots and base words, and for the first time, some common Latin phrases are included.

Have the students first sort the words by their root, *bene* or *mal*. Begin your discussion by asking the students which words they think they know the meaning of, and discuss these. Be sure to elicit from the students the realization that *benefit* has to do with "good." Discuss *malfunction*—if something *malfunctions* does it function well or poorly? Then discuss *benefactor*: Do the students recognize another root they've recently explored (*-fac-* in Sort 34, "to make")? A *benefactor*, then, is literally someone who "makes good," or is *beneficial* and *benevolent*—which literally means "good will" (*vol* = "will"). Contrast *benefactor* with *malefactor*. *Benediction* contains not only the root *dic*, but the root *bene* as well, meaning "good." So, *benediction* literally means "good saying" and usually refers to the blessing at the end of many religious services.

Then introduce the prefixes *ante-* and *post-*. Tell the students that they are likely to run into several *ante* and *post* words and phrases in their history books. *Antebellum* and *postbellum* literally mean "before the war" and "after the war." In America, *antebellum* most often refers to the time period before the Civil War, as in *antebellum* architecture or *antebellum* attitudes and beliefs. Students have probably heard of *ante meridian* and *post meridian*—if not, ask them what they think "AM" and "PM" refer to. Share that *meridian* is a Latin word meaning "midday." *Anterior* and *posterior* refer to "before, in front" and "behind, in back," respectively. Tell them that *postscript* is also commonly represented with initials (p.s.). (Students may be familiar with the euphemistic use of *posterior* to refer to one's rear end!)

bene	mal	ante-	post-
benefit	**malfunction**	**antebellum**	**postpone**
beneficial	malevolent	ante meridian	post meridian
benefactor	dismal	antedate	postbellum
benevolent	malaria	anterior	postmortem
benediction	malcontent		posterior
	malefactor		postscript
	malice		
	malicious		
	maladroit		

Extend

Remind students of the name of one of Harry Potter's classmates, Malfoy. J. K. Rowling has created many of the characters' names using Greek and Latin elements. Challenge students to brainstorm other names from the series that give a clue to the personality of the character.

Additional Words.   *benefactress, beneficiary, benevolence, malady, malaise, malapropism, malediction, malformation, malfeasance, malformed, malign, malignant, malinger, malnourished, malpractice, maltreated, antecedent, antechamber, antepenult, anteroom, postdated, postgraduate, posthumous, postnasal, postpaid*

SORT 37   GREEK AND LATIN ELEMENTS: AMOUNTS (*MAGNI, MIN, POLY, EQU, OMNI*)

(See page 107.) This sort examines the meanings of the elements *magni*, which means "great"; *min* which means "small"; *poly*, which means "much" or "many"; *equ*, which means "equal"; and *omni*, which means "all."

Although the meanings of these Greek elements are fairly straightforward, their combination with other elements to form the words in this sort may be a bit opaque. If you wish, you may walk the students through this sort, sharing as much of the following background information as you believe may be helpful.

Background Information

The Greek combining forms usually occur as prefixes and in a very large number of words. So, too, do the Latin prefixes *equ* and *omni*. For example, *magnificent* includes the Latin root *fic*, which is actually another form of the Latin root *fac* ("make") that was explored in Sort 34. So, *magnificent* literally means "to make great."

Begin the discussion on the prefix *poly* with the word *polysyllabic*, which refers to a word that has three or more syllables. Students will probably be familiar with *polygon* (*gon* meaning "angle"); the other *poly* words are probably less familiar to them. *Polyglot* refers to a person—one who knows many languages (*glot* comes from a Greek word meaning "tongue, language"). *Equ* is fairly straightforward. Begin your discussion with *unequal* and students will quickly determine the meaning of the root. Use a map or globe to point out the *equator*, discuss its meanings, and then discuss *equatorial*, which means having to do with or characterizing the equator. An *equation* has to do with things being equal. Discuss what an *equitable* solution refers to. *Equanimity* may be a new term, meaning, literally, "even (equal)-tempered"; so, if someone possesses *equanimity*, he is calm and even tempered. The end of this word, *animity*, comes from the Latin *animus*, meaning "mind," which in turn is related to Latin *anima* ("life, soul"). This root also occurs in *animal* and *animated* ("living"). Students will probably know the meaning of *equivalent*, but point out that it is made up of *equ-* + *valent*, which comes from the Latin root for "force"—literally, "equal force."

In introducing *omnivore*, ask students if they know the terms *carnivore* and *herbivore*. Then, ask them what an *omnivore* might be. Next, write *science* on the board and ask the students if it gives any clue to *omniscient*. Then tell them that *science* comes from a Latin word meaning "to know." So, *omniscient* means "all knowing." *Conscience* literally means "with knowledge" as in "you knew better but did it anyway."

Demonstrate, Sort, and Reflect

Have the students sort the words by elements, discussing the meaning of the words they know and working to infer the meaning of the remainder. They may check their hypotheses in their dictionaries.

magni	min	poly	equ	omni
magnificent	**miniscule**	**polysyllabic**	**unequal**	**omnipotent**
magnification	minute	polygon	equitable	omnivore
magnitude	diminish	polyglot	equation	omniscient
	minimum	polytechnic	equanimity	
	minnow	polygamy	equator	
	mince		equilateral	
			equivalent	

Extend

Note that the word *minute* is a homophone that can be pronounced with a long *i* or a short *i*.

Additional Words. *magnify, minimize, minor, minus, minimum, polychrome, polyester, polyhedron, polymath, polymer, polysaccharide, polysemous, polytheism, polyunsaturated, equal, equality, equatorial, equity, equilibrium, equivocate, equidistant, equinox, inequity, omnipresent, omnidirectional*

SORT 38   GREEK AND LATIN ELEMENTS: RELATED TO THE BODY (*CAP, CORP, DENT/DONT, PED/POD*)

(See page 108.) This sort explores roots related to the body: *cap*, which can mean "head," *dent* or *dont* which means "tooth," *corp*, which means "body," and *ped* or *pod*, which means "foot." Note that *cap* can also mean "to take" or "seize" as in *captive*, and *ped* can also refer to a "child" as in *pediatrician*. However, words in which those roots mean "head" or "foot" are more common.

Sort and Reflect

Have students sort the words according to word root. Ask students what *decapitate* means. Their mentioning of "head" allows you to discuss *capital* and *capitol*—these words have to do with "head" of government. But why the difference in spelling? *Capital* refers to the city where the government is located, *capitol* refers to the actual building in which the legislative body of the government meets.

Address the root *corp* by first discussing *corpse*, quite literally, "a body." Move then to *corps*, which is a military unit or body, or a group such as a *press corps*. Then discuss how *corporal* and *corporation* reflect the concept of "body." The primary meaning of *corporal* is "having to do with the body"; another meaning, of course, is the designation of a particular rank in the military.

Students should readily identify with *dentist* and *orthodontist*. Ask students what orthodontists do and explain that *ortho* means "straight or right." Establish that *dent* and *dont* are two versions of the same root. *Peri*, if you recall, means "around" as in *periscope*, so "around the teeth" refers to the gums where periodontal disease may occur. *Indent* is interesting. If you bit something you might leave a dent. The word *dent* means "to notch or bend inward." When you indent a paragraph you might, in a sense, take a bite into it.

Explain that *pod* and *ped* mean the same thing and have students combine them into one column. Have students read through the words to see if they can get a sense of what the root might mean. Ask how *pedal* and *pedicure* might be related. *Pedicure* has two roots; *cure* means "care of." *Expedite* means "to speed up, or execute more quickly." In Latin the root literally meant "to free from entanglements," and going back further to Indo-European, "to free one's foot from a snare." Similarly, *impede* has evolved to mean "obstruct the progress of" something. The meaning of *podium* and *pedestal*, "base," evolved from "foot." Now that they know what *ortho* means ask them to speculate about the meaning of the word *orthopedic*. Based on what they know about *dentist* and *orthodontist*, what might a *podiatrist* do?

cap	corp	dent/dont	ped/pod
decapitate	**corpse**	**dentist**	**pedal**
capitol	corps	orthodontist	pedicure
capital	corpulent	periodontal	pedestal
capitalization	corporal	dentures	centipede
captain	corporation	indent	impede
			orthopedic
			podiatrist
			podium
			pedestrian

Extend

Help students develop a mnemonic strategy to remembering that *capitol* refers to a building. Most capitol buildings have a dome over a rotunda. *Capitol, dome,* and *rotunda* all have an *o* and are round. Look up and discuss other meanings for the word *capital*.

Word hunts may prove challenging for roots like *cap* and *ped* because the letter strings show up in so many words. Students will need to avoid the inflected form in words like *skipped*, and many words have a *cap* chunk that is unrelated to head (*capsize*, *handicap*).

Additional Words.   *per capita, impede, corpus, incorporate, corpuscle, pedometer, quadruped, pedigree, biped, millipede, moped, arthropod, tripod, chiropodist*

SORT 39   GREEK AND LATIN ROOTS (*TERR, ASTR/ASTER, AER, HYDRA/HYDRO*)

(See page 109.) This sort explores the Latin root *terr* meaning "earth" and three Greek roots: *aster* or *astr* meaning "star," *aer* meaning "air," and *hydra* or *hydro* meaning "water."

Students should sort by roots and use their knowledge of known words and prefixes to arrive at some conclusions about what the roots mean. What could a terrier have to do with the earth? *Terriers* are little dogs used to hunt rats and other rodents and willingly dig holes in the earth to catch them. *Astronaut* has the root *naut* which refers to sailing (*nautical*) and sailors, so an astronaut is literally a star sailor! The *naut* root shows up again in *aeronaut*—one who sails through the air in a balloon. The word *disaster* will not be easily related to the other words. Literally it means ill-starred. The ancient Greeks believed that the future could be told through the study of the stars (*astrology*) so a disaster should be foretold in the stars.

terr	astr/aster	aer	hydra/hydro
terrain	**astronomy**	**aerosol**	**dehydrated**
territory	astronaut	aerial	hydrant
terrarium	astrology	aerobatics	hydraulic
subterranean	asteroid	aerobics	hydrogen
terrier	asterisk	aeronaut	hydrate
extraterrestrial	disaster	aerospace	hydrofoil

Additional Words.   *Mediterranean, terrestrial, terrace, terra firma, terracotta, territorial, aster, astronomical, astrophysics, aerate, aerodynamics, aerometer, aeronautics, anaerobic, carbohydrate, dehydrate, hydra, hydroelectric, hydrology, hydroplane, hydroponics, hydrocephalic, hydroxide, hydrolysis, hydrangea, hydrophobia*

SORT 40   LATIN ROOTS (*GEN, MORT, BIO*)

(See page 110.) This sort contrasts *gen*, which means "birth" or "beginning" as well as family, *mort* which means "death," and *bio* meaning "life."

Background Information

The root *gen* occurs in a surprisingly large number of words, and although its meaning has been extended metaphorically, it usually retains at its core the sense of "birth or beginning." We speak of the *genesis* of an idea or event (as well as the first book of the Old Testament and the Torah, something students often haven't realized). The root *gen* has this straightforward meaning in *generate* and *regenerate*. The word *progeny* refers to offspring, literally or metaphorically, as with the *progeny* of an artistic movement begun by an earlier artist. *Genetic* derives from *gene*, which also refers to "beginning." The root *gen* has extended in its meaning to refer to "kind," as with *generic*, which refers to a *general* category; *genre*, which refers to a class or type of literature, music, or art, and so forth.

One who is *mortal* must eventually die, but one who is *immortal* will not, and if you feel *mortified* perhaps you wish you could die. The word *mortgage* has no literal connection to death but *gage* refers to a pledge. We are responsible for a mortgage payment even after death.

Sort and Reflect

Have students work in pairs to group the words by root, then discuss their possible meanings. Students will have at least heard most of the words, though they may be uncertain about their meanings. Students may check these words in their dictionaries. Help students recall elements from earlier sorts such as the *logy* in *biology*, *graph* in *biography* and *autobiography*, and the suffix *-ian* (one who does something) in *mortician*.

gen	mort	bio
generate	**mortal**	**biology**
genesis	immortal	microbiology
progenitor	mortician	biodegradable
generic	mortified	antibiotic
genre	mortgage	amphibious
regenerate		biography
progeny		autobiography
genetic		biome
gene		biotic
generation		

Extend

On an etymological note, you can share with the students that *bioscope* was the name for an early movie projector. How do they think this word came about?

Additional Words.   *degenerate, engender, Genesis, genealogy, general, generality, generator, genitals, gentry, miscegenation, immortality, mortuary, rigor mortis, mortify, biochemistry, biofeedback, biogenesis, biological, biomass, biomedical, biopsy, biorhythm, biosphere, macrobiotic, symbiotic, symbiosis*

SORT 41   LATIN ROOTS (*VEN/VENT, JUNCT, SPIR, SEC/SECT*)

(See page 111.) This sort discusses the Latin roots *ven/vent*, meaning "to come"; *junct*, meaning "to join"; *spir*, meaning "to breathe"; and *sec/sect*, "to cut."

Sort and Reflect

Have students sort the words according to the root in each. Follow up by having students discuss, in pairs, how they think the word parts combine to produce the meaning of each word. Have students check the inferred meaning of each root by looking up challenging words in the dictionary.

In most of the *spir* words, the combination of the root and affixes results in a more metaphorical or connotative meaning. *Expire*, for example, literally means "to breathe out," but for the last time. *Conspire*, literally meaning "to breathe with," reflects a close relationship between individuals *(conspiracy)*. The word *insect* may seem a strange match with the others but insects are segmented into three body parts.

ven/vent	junct	spir	sec/sect
convene	**junction**	**perspire**	**dissect**
convention	juncture	respiration	section
intervene	adjunct	inspiration	insect
intervention	conjunction	aspiration	intersection
avenue		conspiracy	sectarian
preventive		transpire	
		expire	
		spiritual	
		dispirited	

Extend

Students might wonder why there is only a single *s* in *dispirited* instead of two as in *misspelled*. Compliment them if they notice it but it is a word that does not follow the generalization of honoring both the base word and the prefix in spelling.

Additional Words.   *adventure, circumvent, convenient, event, eventful, invent, prevention, revenue, souvenir, vent, ventilate, venture, venue, injunction, disjunction, antiperspirant, aspire, aspirate, inspire, perspiration, respiratory, spiracle, spirited, bisect, bisection, dissection, sectional, intersect, sectarianism, sectional, sectionalism, sector, sect, trisect, vivisection*

SORT 42   LATIN ROOTS (*JUD, LEG, MOD, BIBLIO*)

(See page 112.) This sort explores the Latin roots *jud*, meaning "to judge"; *leg*, meaning "law" or "to read"; *mod*, meaning "measure or manner of doing"; and *biblio*, meaning "book." Because of the nature of these roots and their combinations, a substantial amount of background information is included below as part of a more explicit explanation.

Sort and Reflect

Have the students sort the words according to roots, discuss them with a partner, and afterwards share any uncertainties they have about how particular words should be categorized. For example, the *leg* root may not be obvious in *privilege* and *allegiance*.

Ask the students what they think the root *jud* means, and if they are uncertain, write the word *judge* on the board. Then, discuss how *prejudice* literally means "judge before"—people who are *prejudiced* have already judged another person or idea, for example. When a judge *adjudicates* a case she "hears and settles" the case; literally, the word *adjudicate* means "to judge to or toward" something (*ad-* is a prefix meaning "to or toward").

Next, discuss the *biblio* words. Students may have a good idea about the meaning of this root. Begin with *bibliography*, a written list of books. Students may note that *biblical* is related to *Bible*—perhaps the first time they may have thought about the word *Bible* meaning "book." *Bibliophile* offers an opportunity to mention the Greek combining form *phile*, which means "having a strong preference for, loving." Some examples include *Philadelphia*, "city of love," and *anglophile*, someone who loves England and things English. Students who are studying Spanish or whose first language is Spanish will notice the relationship of this word to the word for "library" in Spanish—*biblioteca*.

Have the students work in pairs to sort words that have the *leg* root into two categories: words that have to do with *law* and words that have to do with *reading* or literacy. This process will not be entirely straightforward, so after they have sorted and discussed the words, bring the students back together and do a group sort. Discuss words about which they are uncertain, and if necessary share with them the following information: *Legend* and *legible* and *legion* come from an Indo-European root that means "to gather or collect." If something is *legible*, one can *read* it, "gathering or collecting" information; *legend* comes from a Latin word meaning something that was "to be read," referring to written stories. *Privilege* actually contains two roots—*priv* ("single, alone" as in *private*) and *leg*—and it means, literally, "law for an individual." Have them label their headers to distinguish them in future sorts.

Moderate relates to "measure" in that it refers to keeping within reasonable limits, as when one is a *moderate* eater or eats *moderately*. If you prefer a particular manner or style of learning something, for example, this is often referred to as a preference for a particular *modality*. The most common meaning for *mode* is the "manner" of doing something, which in fact is a meaning that goes back to the Latin word for *mode*—"manner" or "style." Interestingly, this meaning applies to *modern* as well: "in a certain manner, just now."

jud	leg	leg	biblio	mod
prejudice	**legalistic**	**legible**	**bibliography**	**moderate**
adjudicate	legislate	legend	bibliophile	mode
judiciary	allegiance	illegible	biblical	modern
misjudge	privilege			remodel
judgment	legally			modality
	legacy			modification
	delegate			

Extend

Note that *moderate* can be both a verb and a noun and the pronunciation will change accordingly: "Mr. Williams has *moderate* views on remodeling the legal system and will *moderate* a panel discussion next week."

Additional Words.   *judgmental, judicial, injudicious, allege, allegedly, illegal, legally, legacy, legation, legislature, legislation, legislator, legitimate, paralegal, relegate, accommodate, immoderate, modest, immodest, model, modernity, moderator, modicum, modify, modulate, outmoded, a la mode*

ASSESSMENT 6 FOR SORTS 35–42

Use the form on page 113 to assess students' knowledge of root meanings. Ask them to write the letter of the correct match. On the following page is the answer key.

1. ver (d)	a. bad		1. duc (e)	a. flow
2. mal (a)	b. breathe		2. sect (h)	b. small
3. ante (f)	c. all		3. flu (a)	c. death
4. spir (b)	d. turn		4. gen (l)	d. judge
5. omni (c)	e. foot		5. sequ (i)	e. lead
6. poly (j)	f. before		6. hydra (g)	f. land
7. cap (i)	g. good		7. min (b)	g. water
8. ped (e)	h. life		8. dent (j)	h. cut
9. bene (g)	i. head		9. mort (c)	i. follow
10. corp (k)	j. many		10. terra (f)	j. tooth
11. astr (l)	k. body		11. jud (d)	k. turn
12. bio (h)	l. star		12. ver (k)	l. birth

Ask students to spell and define the following words.

1. consecutive	2. affluence	3. beneficial	4. malevolent	5. omnivore
6. corporal	7. aerosol	8. hydraulic	9. conspiracy	10. sectarian
11. judiciary	12. privilege	13. vertigo	14. anterior	15. equation
16. terrarium	17. asteroid	18. antibiotic	19. progeny	20. allegiance

SORT 35   Latin Roots (*duc/duct, sequ/sec, flu, ver/vert*)

duc/duct	*sequ/sec*	*flu*	*ver/vert*
introduction		**sequel**	**fluid**
reverse		induce	inverse
fluent		consequence	convert
extravert		conductor	educate
influx		subsequent	sect
vertigo		superfluous	abduct
reduce		conversation	affluence
fluctuate		consecutive	deduct

SORT 36   Latin Roots (*bene*, *mal*) and Prefixes (*ante-*, *post-*)

bene	*mal*	*ante-*	*post-*
benefit	**malfunction**		**antebellum**
postpone	beneficial		malevolent
dismal	ante meridian		benefactor
anterior	post meridian		malaria
malice	benediction		postmortem
postscript	posterior		malefactor
malicious	benevolent		maladroit
postbellum	malcontent		antedate

SORT 37   Greek and Latin Elements: Amounts (*magni*, *min*, *poly*, *equ*, *omni*)

magni	*min*	*poly*	*equ*	*omni*

magnificent	**polysyllabic**	**miniscule**
unequal	**omnipotent**	minimum
polygon	magnification	equitable
magnitude	polytechnic	polyglot
omnivore	equanimity	diminish
minute	equilateral	equation
polygamy	omniscient	equator
minnow	equivalent	mince

SORT 38   Greek and Latin Elements: Related to the Body
(cap, corp, dent/dont, ped/pod)

cap	*corp*	*dent/dont*	*ped/pod*
decapitate	**corpse**		**dentist**
pedal	orthodontist		capital
corps	pedestrian		pedicure
pedestal	capitalization		impede
capitol	periodontal		corpulent
podiatrist	corporation		dentures
corporal	centipede		captain
indent	orthopedic		podium

SORT 39   Greek and Latin Roots (*terr*, *astr/aster*, *aer*, *hydra/hydro*)

terr	*astr/aster*	*aer*	*hydra/hydro*
terrain	**astronomy**		**aerosol**
dehydrated	aerobics		aeronaut
astronaut	terrarium		territory
aerial	aerobatics		hydraulic
hydrant	hydrogen		asteroid
terrier	subterranean		astrology
hydrate	aerospace		asterisk
disaster	extraterrestrial		hydrofoil

SORT 40   Latin Roots (*gen, mort, bio*)

gen	*mort*	*bio*
generate	**mortal**	**biology**
immortal	microbiology	genesis
generic	progenitor	mortician
antibiotic	mortified	genre
progeny	biodegradable	biography
amphibious	regenerate	genetic
gene	generation	biome
biotic	autobiography	mortgage

SORT 41   Latin Roots (*ven/vent*, *junct*, *spir*, *sec/sect*)

ven/vent	*junct*	*spir*	*sec/sect*
convene	**junction**		**perspire**
dissect	convention		spiritual
expire	respiration		juncture
intervene	conspiracy		inspiration
dispirited	intersection		adjunct
aspiration	intervention		transpire
avenue	conjunction		insect
sectarian	preventive		section

SORT 42   Latin Roots (*jud*, *leg*, *mod*, *biblio*)

jud	*leg*	*leg*	*mod*	*biblio*
prejudice		**legalistic**		**legible**
moderate		**bibliography**		legislate
legend		remodel		adjudicate
modern		allegiance		mode
judiciary		bibliophile		privilege
modality		judgment		illegible
legally		delegate		misjudge
legacy		modification		biblical

ASSESSMENT 6 FOR SORTS 35–42
Beside each root write the letter of the matching meaning.

Name _____

a. flow	1. duc	
b. small	2. sect	
c. death	3. flu	
d. judge	4. gen	
e. lead	5. sequ	
f. land	6. hydra	
g. water	7. min	
h. cut	8. dent	
i. follow	9. mort	
j. tooth	10. terra	
k. turn	11. jud	
l. birth	12. ver	

a. bad	1. ver	
b. breathe	2. mal	
c. all	3. ante	
d. turn	4. spir	
e. foot	5. omni	
f. before	6. poly	
g. good	7. cap	
h. life	8. ped	
i. head	9. bene	
j. many	10. corp	
k. body	11. astr	
l. star	12. bio	

Unit VII   Greek and Latin Elements III

NOTES FOR THE TEACHER

See the teacher notes on page 69 (Greek and Latin Elements I) which still apply here. Many of the Greek and Latin elements explored in these sorts are more "connotative" than literal in their function. As with a number of the roots in the last unit, however, it may often still be helpful to walk through the literal meaning of the combination of these elements, as students may then understand and appreciate how the meaning has evolved. When students understand the finer shades of meaning and connotation that elements at this level reflect, they are very well prepared to dissect, analyze, and reconstruct unfamiliar words they will encounter in their reading and study across a wide range of content domains. Importantly, the types of attention given to word study at this level are similar to the types of thinking required for understanding and acquiring another language.

In many instances reference is made to the Indo-European root to which a particular Latin root may be traced. Although exploration of Indo-European roots is not emphasized in these sorts, the occasional mention here offers students an intriguing glimpse into more advanced word study. Now that it is easier to access the *Dictionary of Indo-European Roots* either on CD or online (www.bartleby.com/61/IEroots.html), the potential for more students to pursue word etymology is promising.

SORT 43   GREEK AND LATIN ROOTS (*VOC/VOKE, LING/LANG, MEM, PSYCH*)

(See page 123.) The roots in this sort refer to language or to the mind: *ling* means "language"; *voc* means "voice" or "call"; *mem* comes from Latin for "mind"; and *psych* comes from Greek for "mind" or "mental."

Background Information

Begin with *voc* and the words in which the meaning of the root and its function are straightforward: *vocal* (characterizing or having to do with the voice) and *vocabulary*. Share with the students that *advocate* literally means "speaking to" or "toward" something, which is what an *advocate* does or what you do when you *advocate* for someone. *Provoke,* literally meaning "to call forth," has taken on a metaphorical meaning; to bring forth anger, for example. People often feel that their *vocation* is a "calling."

You may wish to discuss the spelling-meaning relationship among the words *provoke/provocation/provocative,* noting the sound and spelling changes across the words. *Invoke* literally means "to call in" or, more metaphorically, to call upon another for help. In the related words *provocation* and *invocation,* the spelling of *voc* changes; in English spelling, *-oce* is not an allowable word-final spelling pattern, but *-oke* is.

Remind students of the words *bilingual* and *monolingual;* what, then, does *multilingual* mean? The root *ling* refers to "language," but point out to the students that it originally meant "tongue" in Latin; the extension to language more generally was quite natural. Words with the *ling* root offer some good possibilities for exploration: A *linguist* is one who studies language, After discussing these *ling* words, ask the students why they think *linguini* has the *ling* root. You may need to remind them of the original Latin meaning for *ling,* "tongue"; so the meaning of *linguini,* therefore, returns us to "having to do with the tongue"! You may use this opportunity to remind students that English shares a number of roots with other languages, and *linguini* is a great example of this.

The root *mem* is fairly straightforward. *Memory* has to do, obviously, with the mind. *Remember* literally means bringing the mind "back." *Commemorate* has to do with honoring the memory of someone—remembering "with" (*com*) others. Discuss *immemorial* by introducing this sentence: "Since time *immemorial,* people have said that dogs are humans' best friend." Discuss how the meaning "without memory" literally refers to a time beyond anyone's memory. (Note: A spelling hint for the *mem* words. Often students are uncertain whether to double the *m* in words such as *commemorate* and *immemorial.* Remind them that they should always first think of such words in terms of the base word or root—*memory* or *mem*—and prefixes that are added to the base or root.) Note that the familiar term *memo* is short for *memorandum.*

The root *psych* may be known to students as the slang expression to "psyche someone out" or to be "psyched about doing something," but they may not have related it to *psychology* or the "study of the mind."

Demonstrate, Sort, and Reflect

Prepare a set of words to use for teacher-directed modeling. Save the discussion of word meanings until after sorting. Display a transparency of the words on the overhead or hand out the sheet of words to the students. Ask them what they notice about the words and get ideas about how the words can be sorted. Students usually notice that all the words contain roots. Have students work in pairs to group the words by roots, then discuss their possible meanings. Students will have at least heard most words, though they may be uncertain about their meanings. Students may check these words in their dictionaries. Share the background knowledge above.

voc/voke	ling/lang	mem	psych
vocal	**linguist**	**memory**	**psychology**
vocalize	lingo	memorial	psychiatrist
provocative	language	remember	psyche
advocate	linguini	commemorate	psyched
invoke	multilingual	memorandum	
vocation	slang	immemorial	
provoke		memento	

Extend

The suffix *-ate,* which often signals a verb, was briefly introduced in Sort 16 and can be reviewed here. *Advocate* is either a verb or a noun depending on the sound of the vowel in the final syllable. You might *advocate* (/ate/) for change in which case you are an *advocate* (/it/). There are additional words ending in *-ate* that work the same way. The verbs always end in /ate/ while the nouns or adjectives end in /it/: *affiliate, alternate, approximate, associate, degenerate, deliberate, dominate, duplicate, estimate, graduate, lubricate, moderate, participate, separate,* and *subordinate.* Understanding how these pairs work can help students remember to add the final *e* when they spell the words even when the vowel in the last syllable is not long.

Additional Words.   *vociferous, evoke, convocation, equivocal, irrevocable, provocateur, revoke, unequivocable, vocalic, vocalist, vocational, sociolinguist, bilingual, linguistics, memo, memoir, memorabilia, memorable, memorize, remembrance, parapsychology, psychopathology, psycholinguistics, psychedelic, psychiatic, psychoanalysis, psychotherapy, psychologist, psychopath, psychosis, psychotic*

SORT 44   GREEK AND LATIN ROOTS (*PATH, SENS/SENT, MED/MEDI, SOL*)

(See page 124.) This sort introduces *path* meaning "disease or suffering"; *sens/sent*, meaning "sense"; *med/medi*, meaning "heal"; and *sol*, meaning "alone."

Sort and Reflect

As with the previous sort, this sort provides an excellent opportunity to walk through the words and elements explicitly.

Have students sort the words by root. Then, discuss the meaning of each. The root *path* is a good example of metaphorical extension: The original root in Greek meant "suffering," but became extended to mean *disease,* and *feeling* or *emotion,* and it is in the latter sense that it functions in words such as *sympathy* and *empathy*. Mention that *sympathy/sympathetic* and *empathy/empathetic* are often confused: You are *empathetic* if you truly feel like someone else is feeling and you have experienced what they are experiencing; you are *sympathetic* if you feel sorry for them. Have students dissect and discuss the literal meanings of *apathy, telepathy,* and *antipathy* ("without feeling," "feeling from far away," "feeling against").

Interestingly, *med/medi* ("to heal") came from the same Indo-European root that had to do with "measuring." When a doctor attempts to heal someone, she literally "takes appropriate measures." Have students dissect *remedy* and *remedial* ("to heal again"). *Medevac* is a "blended" form constructed from *medical* and *evacuation*. The root *sens/sent* refers to "feeling" and has evolved to refer to "opinion" as well. With this in mind, have students analyze the *sens/sent* words. After discussing the meaning of *solo,* have students suggest the possible meaning of the root *sol*. Extend this discussion to the other *sol* words.

path	sens/sent	med/medi	sol
sympathy	**sensation**	**medicine**	**solo**
apathy	sensational	remedy	soliloquy
telepathy	sentiment	remedial	solitaire
antipathy	dissent	medevac	desolate
empathy	sensitivity	medic	solitude
pathetic			isolate
pathology			sole

Extend

Apathy and *telepathy* are nouns. What are their adjectival forms? (*apathetic, telepathic*) How does the sound change across these words?

Additional Words.   *psychopath, homeopathic, pathogen, pathogenic, pathological, pathos, sociopath, sympathize, sympathetic, telepathic, consensual, desensitize, dissension, extrasensory, hypersensitive, insensible, photosensitive, presentment, quintessential, resent, resentful, resentment, sensation, sensationalism, sentient, sensitivity, sensor, sensual, sensuality, sensuous, sentimental, sentiments, medicinal, Medicaid, medical, medicate, medicated, medication, isolation, solitary, soloist*

SORT 45   PREFIXES (*INTRA-*, *INTER-*, *INTRO-*, *CIRCUM-*)

(See page 125.) This sort explores the prefixes *intra-*, meaning "within"; *inter-*, meaning "between" or "among"; *intro-*, meaning "in" or "inward"; and *circum-*, meaning "around."

Demonstrate

Have students sort the words by prefix, and discuss what they think each prefix means. Then do a subsort of words that they know, have heard or seen, or do not know. Explore those about which they have heard or that they do not know.

Ask students what root they see in *introvert*. If necessary, remind them of the *vert/vers* words they examined in Sort 35. This word literally means "to turn inward." Tell the students that *intercept* contains the root *cept*, meaning "to take." Do they see how the prefix and root result in the meaning of "to take in between"? Recall that the root *spect* means "to look"; so if someone engages in *introspection*, they literally "look inward."

Students are familiar with the word *intramural*, but usually have not analyzed it. Ask them to define *mural*, then either tell them or have them look up the Latin meaning of *mural* ("wall"). The word *intramural* has the literal meaning "within the wall," so *intramural* sports are, understandably, within the walls of the same school; *intermural* sports are "between" the walls of different schools.

intra-	*inter-*	*intro-*	*circum-*
intramural	**intermural**	**introvert**	**circumference**
intravenous	interact	introspective	circumnavigate
intrapersonal	international	introduce	circumscribe
intrastate	interpersonal		circumvent
	interstate		circumstance
	intercept		circumspect
	internet		
	interchange		

Additional Words.   *intracellular, interactive, interbred, intercede, interception, intercession, intercommunication, intercom, intercourse, interdependent, interface, interfere, intergalactic, interject, interlock, interloper, interlude, intermediary, intermingle, intermission, interplay, interracial, interrogate, interruption, intersection, interspersed, interstellar, interwoven, circumcise, circumflex, circumpolar, circumstantial*

SORT 46   LATIN ROOTS (*PRESS, PUR/PURG, FUS, PEND*)

(See page 126.) This sort examines *press*, which means "to press"; *purg*, which means "to cleanse"; *fuse*, which means "to pour"; and *pend*, which means "to hang." Students will know most of the words in this sort. The primary objective here is to understand how these particular roots contribute to the meaning of the words in which they occur.

Background Information

Fus is perhaps most interesting in that its meaning ("pour") has become metaphorically extended in a large number of words. Have students analyze and discuss the literal meaning of each of the words (e.g., *transfusion* is literally "to pour across"; *effusive* is literally "to pour out"; *confuse* is "to pour together"). Ask students if *purge* reminds them of a very common word (*pure*). In Christian belief, *purgatory* is a place where the souls of those who have not died "in grace" must linger until they have atoned for, or "purged," of their sins.

Sort and Reflect

Have students sort the words according to the root in each. Follow up by having students discuss, in pairs, how they think the word parts combine to produce the meaning of each word. Have students check the inferred meaning of each root by looking up challenging words in the dictionary.

press	pur/purg	fus	pend
pressure	**purge**	**transfusion**	**pendulum**
oppressive	expurgate	diffuse	suspend
depression	purgatory	confuse	pendant
impressive	Puritan	infusion	impending
espresso	impure	profuse	perpendicular
compression	purification		suspenders
			depend

Additional Words. *antidepressant, compress, decompress, express, expressive, expression, expressway, impress, impression, impressionable, irrepressive, oppress, oppressive, pressurize, repress, repression, suppress, suppression, expurgation, purebred, purgative, purification, purifier, purist, puritanical, confusion, defused, fusion, infuse, profusion, suffuse, append, appendix, compendium, dependent, dependable, impending, independent, pending, pendulous, suspend, suspends*

SORT 47 LATIN ROOTS (*POS, LOC, SIST, STA/STAT/STIT*)

(See page 127.) This sort discusses the Latin roots *pos*, meaning "to put or place"; *loc*, meaning "place"; *sist*, meaning "to stand"; and *sta/stat/stit*, meaning "to stand."

Background Information

Sist and *sta/stat/stit* come from the original Indo-European root *sta*, meaning "to stand" or "to set up." Interestingly, just two letters of this root remain in some words, for example, the *st* in re*st*. The word *rest* literally means "to stand again," being composed of the prefix *re-* and the root *sta*. A striking number of words contain a part that originated with this Indo-European root.

This root provides a good opportunity to talk with students about how the meaning of a word evolves from the combination of the root and affixes that compose it. For example, if something is *constant* it continually "stands with"; *statistics* describe the "state" of things or "where they stand"—people, trends, weather, and so on. In Latin, *sist* means "to stand"; the words *insist* and *persistent*, for example, have the sense of standing firmly. A *constitution* is a document that "sets up" (*stit*) a nation; a *substitute* is someone or something that stands (*stit*) in place of (*sub*); and when someone is granted *restitution* they are literally "set (back) up," usually monetarily.

Demonstrate

Have students sort the words by root, and ask which ones they can guess the meaning of. *Loc-* and possibly *pos-* will be the most obvious to them. Most of us don't realize that *sist* and *sta/stat/stit* are variants of the same root meaning "to stand." Engage the students in analyzing the words containing these roots and then checking them with the dictionary. This is a good opportunity to discuss the prefix *ob-*, meaning "against."

pos	loc	sist	sta/stat/stit
position	**locate**	**insistent**	**instability**
deposit	relocate	persistent	stationary
compose	location	resistance	statue
disposable	locomotion	consistent	obstacle
proposal	dislocate		establish
repository			substitute
composite			constitution
			institution

Extend

Have students be on the lookout for *sist* and *sta/stat/stit* in their reading and record examples in their vocabulary notebooks.

Additional Words. *composition, compost, composure, decompose, deposition, depository, dispose, disposal, expose, expository, juxtapose, oppose, opposite, pose, possess, possession, predispose, preposition, proposition, superimpose, repose, suppose, suppository, transpose, allocate, collocate, echolocate, locale, locality, locate, location, locomotive, locomotor, subsist, assist, assistance, desist, resist, constant, station, statistic, constituent, institutional, prostitute, restitution, substitution, superstition*

SORT 48   LATIN ROOTS (*CED/CESS/CEED, TEN/TEND, LIT*)

(See page 128.) The root *-ced-/-cess-/-ceed* means "to go," and its spelling changes depending on the words in which it occurs. The Indo-European root *ten* originally meant "to stretch" or "to be pulled," but has also come to mean "to hold." The later meaning will be further covered in the next sort. *Lit* means "letter." *Obliterate* (literally "write against") means "to erase or rub off so as to leave no trace."

Demonstrate

ced/cess/ceed	ten/tend	lit
proceed	**tension**	**literature**
procession	extend	literate
recede	extension	alliteration
recession	tenuous	illiterate
exceed	tendon	literal
precede	tendril	obliterate
secede	distended	
secession	tendency	
succeed	hypertension	

Additional Words. *intercede, intercession, access, accessible, exceed, excess, excessive, inaccessible, process, recess, recessional, distend, extendable, tendonitis, extensively, hypertension, tensile, literary, literally, literati, obliteration*

Extend

Review the sound and spelling changes when /shun/ is added to words that end in *d*: *recede/recession, proceed /procession, secede/secession, extend/extension.* Observe that *proceed, exceed,* and *succeed* are the only words in which the spelling of the root *ced* is *ceed.* Both *ceed* and *cede* change to *cess* before *-ion.* This is another predictable spelling change to add to the *-ion* chart.

Contrast the sound of *-ate* in *obliterate* and *literate. Obliterate* is a verb and *literate* is an adjective.

SORT 49   PREDICTABLE SPELLING CHANGES IN WORD ROOTS (*CEIV/CEP, TAIN/TEN, NOUNCE/NUNC*)

(See page 129.) This sort examines the word roots *ceiv/cep,* meaning "to take"; *tain/ten,* meaning "to hold"; and *nounce/nunc,* meaning "to report."

Background Information

The words in this sort illustrate that the spelling in semantically related words can change, but when it does, it does so predictably. For example, when examining words one at a time one may question why the spelling of the root changes. In this sort, the spelling change is significant; but when the words are grouped in spelling-meaning families, students can see how this change is predictable. Adding suffixes to words such as *deceive, detain,* and *pronounce* changes the spelling in these words in a pattern that is predictable and applies to other words with these roots.

Sort and Reflect

Have students sort the words according to the root in each. Follow up by having students discuss, in pairs, how they think the word parts combine to produce the meaning of each word. When we *deceive* someone we ensnare them or take them under false pretenses. When we *conceive* an idea we are "taken with it." The *tain/ten* words are easier to connect with the idea of "holding" and *nounce/nunc* seems to be easier to understand as "speaking."

ceiv/cep	tain/ten	nounce/nunc
deceive	**container**	**announce**
preconceive	detain	pronounce
deception	attend	denounce
conceive	abstain	pronunciation
conception	obtain	renounce
preconception	retention	denunciation
	detention	announcement
	attention	renunciation
	abstention	
	retain	

Extend

Pull out derived forms with *-ion* together with the base word: *deceive/deception, conceive/conception, abstain/abstention, detain/detention, renounce/renunciation, pronounce/pronunciation*. Talk about the spelling and sound changes in each pair. List these words and ask students to turn the verbs into nouns by adding *-ion*: *perceive, receive*. List these with other predictable spelling changes before *-ion*.

The rule of "*i* before *e* except after *c*" applies in the spelling of *deceive, perceive*, and other *ceive* words.

Additional Words.   *conceivable, inconceivable, misconceive, concept, conception, conceptualize, perceive, perceivable, perception, perceptual, receive, reception, receptacle, receptionist, attendance, bartender, contain, containment, superintend, intent, maintain, maintenance, obtain, portent, pertain, sustenance, tenure, tenacity, tenacious, tenable, announcer, enunciate, mispronounce, pronouncement*

ASSESSMENT 7 FOR SORTS 43–49

Use the form on page 130 to assess students' knowledge of the roots covered in this unit. Below is the answer key.

1. voc (h)	a. mind		1. ling (d)	a. hang
2. intra (d)	b. alone		2. pend (a)	b. stretch, hold
3. sens (j)	c. stand		3. lit (j)	c. around
4. purg (e)	d. within		4. psych (f)	d. language
5. pos (g)	e. cleanse		5. circum (c)	e. report
6. mem (a)	f. between		6. med (k)	f. mind
7. path (i)	g. place		7. fus (g)	g. pour
8. sol (b)	h. voice		8. loc (i)	h. stand
9. inter (f)	i. suffer		9. tend (b)	i. place
10. stat (c)	j. sense		10. nounce (e)	j. letters
11. ced/cess (l)	k. hold		11. ceive (l)	k. heal
12. ten/tain (k)	l. go		12. sist (h)	l. take

Ask students to spell and define the following words.

1. advocate	2. memorandum	3. solitaire
4. psychology	5. empathy	6. persistent
7. intervene	8. aversion	9. introspective
10. expurgate	11. impending	12. obstacle
13. precede	14. secession	15. announce

SORT 43   Greek and Latin Roots (*voc/voke, ling/lang, mem, psych*)

voc/voke	*psych*	*mem*	*ling/lang*
vocal	**psychology**		**memory**
linguist	remember		vocalize
advocate	commemorate		lingo
language	psychiatrist		invoke
vocation	memorandum		memorial
psyche	multilingual		provoke
slang	immemorial		linguini
memento	provocative		psyched

SORT 44   Greek and Latin Roots (*path*, *sens/sent*, *med/medi*, *sol*)

path	*sens/sent*	*med/medi*	*sol*
sympathy	**sensation**		**medicine**
solo	soliloquy		apathy
dissent	telepathy		remedy
solitaire	sentiment		antipathy
empathy	desolate		remedial
solitude	sensitivity		pathetic
medevac	pathology		medic
sole	isolate		sensational

SORT 45   Prefixes (*intra-*, *inter-*, *intro-*, *circum-*)

intra-	inter-	intro-	circum-
intramural	**circumference**		**introvert**
introduce	intrapersonal		**intermural**
intrastate	international		intravenous
circumspect	circumnavigate		introspective
interact	circumscribe		circumvent
interstate	interpersonal		intercept
internet	circumstance		interchange

SORT 46   Latin Roots (*press, pur/purg, fus, pend*)

press	*pur/purg*	*fus*	*pend*
pressure	**transfusion**		**purge**
pendulum	expurgate		diffuse
suspend	infusion		purgatory
impure	perpendicular		impressive
depression	suspenders		confuse
profuse	purification		pendant
espresso	impending		Puritan
depend	compression		oppressive

SORT 47   Latin Roots (*pos, loc, sist, sta/stat/stit*)

pos	loc	sist	sta/stat/stit
instability		**position**	**locate**
insistent		constitution	compose
deposit		stationary	relocate
location		persistent	proposal
obstacle		institution	composite
establish		locomotion	resistance
statue		disposable	substitute
repository		consistent	dislocate

SORT 48   Latin Roots (*ced/cess/ceed*, *ten/tend*, *lit*)

ced/cess/ceed	*ten/tend*	*lit*
proceed	**literature**	**tension**
distended	procession	extend
recede	extension	literate
tenuous	alliteration	exceed
precede	obliterate	tendon
illiterate	recession	secede
succeed	hypertension	literal
tendency	secession	tendril

SORT 49   Predictable Spelling Changes in Word Roots
(ceiv/cep, tain/ten, nounce/nunc)

ceiv/cep	nounce/nunc	tain/ten
deceive	**announce**	**container**
attend	preconceive	detain
obtain	pronunciation	conceive
deception	renunciation	abstain
retention	preconception	detention
pronounce	denunciation	denounce
conception	announcement	attention
retain	abstention	renounce

ASSESSMENT 7 FOR SORTS 43–49
Beside each root write the letter of the matching meaning.

Name _____

a. hang	1. ling
b. stretch, hold	2. pend
c. around	3. lit
d. language	4. psych
e. report	5. cicum
f. mind	6. med
g. pour	7. fus
h. stand	8. loc
i. place	9. tend
j. letters	10. nounce
k. heal	11. ceive
l. take	12. sist

a. mind	1. voc
b. alone	2. intra
c. stand	3. sens
d. within	4. purg
e. cleanse	5. pos
f. between	6. mem
g. place	7. path
h. voice	8. sol
i. suffer	9. inter
j. sense	10. stat
k. hold	11. ced/cess
l. go	12. ten/tain

Unit VIII Advanced Spelling-Meaning Patterns

NOTES FOR THE TEACHER

Background and Objectives

The spelling-meaning patterns explored in these sorts address the types of errors that plague more advanced spellers: -ent/-ant and -ence/-ance uncertainties, confusion over -able/-ible, and not knowing when to double the final consonant when adding inflectional endings to words such as benefit. Sort 55 takes a look at words imported from French along with some French spelling patterns. Students will:

- Spell and demonstrate an understanding of the meaning of words, roots, and affixes covered in these sorts
- Spell these words correctly

Targeted Learners

These sorts are designed for students in the late derivational relations stage who are typically in middle school and high school. The focus in this unit returns to spelling issues that plague even the best spellers. The assessment on page 136 can be used as a pretest as well as a posttest.

Teaching Tips

Word hunts through reading materials will be productive for these features because many of them occur in hundreds of words. Make word hunts ongoing so that students continue to add to them over time. Blind sorts with partners will be useful when comparing patterns such as -ent and -ant which sound alike when pronounced naturally.

These sorts offer opportunities to review many affixes and word roots as well as the generalizations that cover the formation of derived forms. If you have been keeping charts of these features continue to refer to them and add to them throughout this unit.

The game Defiance or Patience described in Chapter 8 of WTW is particularly designed to review the -ance and -ence affix.

SORT 50 SUFFIXES (-ENT/-ENCE, -ANT/-ANCE)

(See page 137.) The relationship between -ent/-ence and -ant/-ance is powerful and straightforward. Students' understanding of this relationship, however, depends on considerable experience with these patterns and the words that represent them. Therefore, Sorts 50 and 51 appear at this point in the scope and sequence rather than earlier.

Sort and Reflect

Have students sort the words by pairs; for example, align *confidence* with *confident* and *brilliance* with *brilliant*. Tell the students that by arranging the words this way they will find a clue to the *-ent/-ence* and *-ant/-ance* puzzle.

The key to understanding these suffixes is this: If you know how to spell one word that ends in *-ent* and *-ence* or *-ant* and *-ance*, then you can figure out how to spell the word about which you're uncertain. For example, if you are uncertain whether a spelling is *dependant* or *dependent* but you know how to spell the word *independence*, then *independence* is your clue to the spelling of *dependent: -ent* and *-ence* words go to-gether, and *-ant* and *-ance* words go together. Talk about how *-ent* and *-ant* signal ad-jectives and *-ence* and *-ance* signal nouns. Add these to your chart of suffixes started earlier.

-ent	-ence	-ant	-ance
absent	**absence**	**fragrant**	**fragrance**
confident	confidence	assistant	assistance
patient	patience	dominant	dominance
different	difference	defiant	defiance
obedient	obedience	distant	distance
intelligent	intelligence		
prominent	prominence		

Extend

Share the book *Antics* by Cathi Hepworth which features words with the *ant* sequence illustrated by ants in various roles. Although this is an alphabet book, it is definitely for older students who will appreciate the humor in the illustrations for *deviant* and *flamboyant.*

During word hunts students are likely to find only one of a pair and will need to gen-erate the matching word. Many words like *deodorant, ancient,* or *consent* do not have a corresponding form with *-ance* or *-ence* but students can list them anyway. They should avoid words ending in *-ment* which is a different suffix studied earlier in Sort 8. Have students determine which pattern, *-ent/-ence* or *-ant/-ance*, appears to be the most fre-quent. (It's *-ent/-ence*.)

Additional Words.   *adherent, adherence, adolescent, adolescence, convenient, convenience, excellent, excellence, innocent, innocence, imminent, imminence, impertinent, impertinence, iridescent, iridescence, negligent, negligence, persistent, persistence, present, presence, violent, violence, abundant, abundance, attendant, attendance, ignorant, ignorance, impor-tant, importance, significant, significance, irrelevant, irrelevance, relevant, relevance, tolerant, tolerance*

SORT 51   SUFFIXES (-ENT/-ENCE/-ENCY, -ANT/-ANCE/-ANCY)

(See page 138.) The suffixes from the last sort are reviewed here with words that can also take *-ency* or *-ancy*. These suffixes signal nouns and suggest "the state of" rather than just the thing itself. Students should sort related words and will discover how the *-ency/-ancy* spelling works. Help students identify words that have a base word such as *reside* and *depend.*

-ent/-ence/-ency			-ant/-ance/-ancy		
resident	residence	residency	abundant	abundance	abundancy
competent	competence	competency	brilliant	brilliance	brilliancy
emergent	emergence	emergency	hesitant	hesitance	hesitancy
lenient	lenience	leniency			

Extend

The Defiance or Patience game described in Chapter 8 of *WTW* can be used to reinforce these words and will focus on the base words as well.

Additional Words.   *affluent, affluence, affluency, buoyant, buoyance, buoyancy, competent, competence, competency, consistent, consistence, consistency, excellent, excellence, excellency, expectant, expectance, expectancy, equivalent, equivalence, equivalency, persistent, persistence, persistency, resident, residence, residency, malignant, malignance, malignancy, compliant, compliance, compliancy*

SORT 52   SUFFIXES (-ABLE,-IBLE)

(See page 139.) This sort develops the core understanding that, when adding this suffix to a base word, it often is spelled *-able;* when adding to a word root, it is often spelled *-ible.* There are many exceptions to this generalization but this is a good place to start.

Demonstrate

Have the students sort the *-able* words and the *-ible* words in separate categories. Then, ask them to examine each category to see if they notice a pattern: When is this suffix spelled *-able* and when is it spelled *-ible*? (*-able* is usually added to base words; *-ible* is usually added to word roots.) Help students find the oddballs. Talk about what the addition of the suffix does to the base word. (It changes verbs to adjectives.) Review any roots covered in earlier sorts such as *aud*, *dict*, *tain*, and *pend*.

-able		-ible		oddball
enjoyable	adaptable	**invincible**	intangible	**formidable**
profitable	attainable	edible	terrible	corruptible
predictable	questionable	eligible	feasible	
perishable	decipherable	plausible	compatible	
laughable	sustainable	indelible	combustible	
punishable		reproducible		

Extend

When students go on a word hunt they will find many words that end with these suffixes but not all will fit these two categories. More cases will be examined in the next sort, so for now have students put words like *legible* or *accessible* in the oddball category. There are many more words that end in *-able* than *-ible* and a word hunt will help to establish a best-guess strategy: If in doubt, use *-able*.

Additional Words.   *affordable, agreeable, allowable, avoidable, comfortable, dependable, expandable, favorable, preferable, reasonable, remarkable, respectable, washable, fallible, foible, gullible, horrible, incredible, infallible, irascible, possible, tangible* Oddball: *resistible, memorable, inevitable, digestible, exhaustible, contemptible, permissible*

SORT 53   ADDING *-ABLE* AND *-IBLE* (*E*-DROP AND *Y* TO *I*)

Demonstrate

(See page 140.) Have students sort the words into three columns: words in which the *e* is dropped before adding *-able*, those in which the *e* is kept, and those in which a final *y* changes to an *i*. The key point to understand is that the *e* is kept when omitting it would result in a change in pronunciation. For example, in *noticeable*, the *c* would become hard; in *manageable*, the *g* would also become hard. Separate out the words that drop the final *e* and add *-ible*. Although all these words have a baseword ending in *-se* there are also words that end in *-se* that *-able*. Adding *-able* after an *e*-drop is much more common but there are some words that students will simply need to remember as adding *-ible* after the *e*-drop.

Drop *e*	Keep *e*	*y* to *i*	*e*-drop + *-ible*
reusable	noticeable	reliable	sensible
adorable	replaceable	undeniable	defensible
consumable	enforceable	identifiable	responsible
excusable	salvageable	variable	reversible
valuable	knowledgeable		
undesirable	manageable		
pleasurable	exchangeable		
unimaginable	agreeable		

Additional Words.   *admirable, conceivable, confusable, deplorable, desirable, excusable, immovable, inadvisable, incomparable, inconceivable, incurable, inescapable, inexcusable, invaluable, lovable, notable, opposable, persuadable, recognizable, removable, usable, danceable, balanceable, disagreeable, irreplaceable, peaceable, pronounceable, serviceable, unchangeable, unbelievable, applicable, invariable, unreliable, undeniable, verifiable, collapsible, convincible, deducible, forcible, indefensible, insensible, reducible, submersible*

SORT 54   ACCENT AND DOUBLING

(See page 141.) This sort is illustrated in a teacher script in Chapter 8 of *WTW*.

Background Information

It is helpful to share the story about Noah Webster's influence at this point (see Chapter 8 of *WTW*). When he wrote the first dictionary of American English in 1828, Webster wanted to distinguish American English from British English. In addition to omitting the *u* in words such as *honour* and *colour* and reversing the *re* in *theatre* and *centre*, he changed the rules for "doubling" final consonants. In British English, the final consonant is almost always doubled (*benefitting*, *levelled*), but not (after 1828) in American English!

Sort and Reflect

Review with students the generalization they have learned about doubling the final consonant before suffixes that begin with a vowel as in *shopped*, *shopping*, or *shopper*. If the word ends in a single vowel and a single consonant, then double.

Look over the words in this sort and determine that in all cases the base word ends in a vowel and a consonant and the prefix begins with a vowel. However, the final consonant is not always doubled. To figure out why, have students sort the words into two columns. Ask students how the words in the two columns are different. To help them out, read down the first column and emphasize the accented syllable. Repeat with the second column. Does that give them a clue? Read the words again and underline the accented syllable so that students can see the pattern. The generalization that applies here is, "If the accent in the base word falls on the final syllable, then double the final consonant before adding the suffix. If the accent does not fall on the last syllable, do not double." Pay special attention to words like *conferred* and *conference*. Note how the accent changes in the base word and this determines whether to double or not.

Double		Do Not Double	
omitted	concurring	**orbited**	modeling
propellant	conferred	benefiting	conference
compelling	forbidden	leveled	limited
forgetting	referred	piloting	reference
preferred	repellant	preference	editing
deferred	beginner	deference	canceled

Extend

It is hard to find many instances of two- or three-syllable words that need to be doubled before adding suffixes that start with a vowel. Challenge students to keep their eyes open for others but do not expect them to find many in a word hunt. Share with the students that doubling the final *l* in words ending in *-el*, such as *travelling*, is widely acceptable and that they will see these spellings in books published in Great Britain and the rest of the British Commonwealth.

To extend the generalization ask students to add *-ing* to these words: *begin* (*beginning*), *exhibit* (*exhibiting*), *excel* (*excelling*), *travel* (*traveling*), *omit* (*omitting*), *tinker* (*tinkering*), *rebel* (*rebelling*), *neighbor* (*neighboring*), *commit* (*committing*), *compel* (*compelling*), *regret* (*regretting*), *label* (*labeling*), *occur* (*occurring*).

Additional Words.   *quarreling, unraveled, counseled, plummeting, magnetic, abhorrent, beginning, riveting, inhabited, inhabitant, robotic, civilize, committed, compelled, dispelled, excelled, excellent, excelling, forbidding, omitting, occurred, permitted, permitting, propeller, propelled, rebelling, rebellion, rebelled, libeled*

SORT 55   WORDS FROM FRENCH

(See page 142.) This final sort explores two special spelling patterns that come to us from the French language. Borrowed words such as these often come with their native spelling patterns. Words like *brunette* end in double *tt*, while the single *t* is silent in words like *ballet*. Both of these spelling patterns appear odd and arbitrary until students learn that when their origin is taken into consideration they represent a fairly consistent spelling pattern.

Demonstrate, Sort, and Reflect

There may be a number of new vocabulary words in this sort and students may not know how to pronounce some of them so be ready to lead the sound sort. Ask students what they notice about the spelling of these words and sort them into two categories to begin (-*et* and -*ette*). After sorting by pattern, read the words aloud under -*et* and ask students to pay attention to the final sound of the word. Have the students help you separate the words with silent *t* so that the sort is similar to the one below. Ask students if they have any ideas about where some of these words originate. They may be able to guess that many are French. Confirm this by looking up the words in a dictionary. Many of the etymologies for words ending in -*ette* will mention that the word is a "diminutive" form. A *cassette* is diminutive of *case* (a small case), a *cigarette* is a diminutive of *cigar* (a small cigar). Look for interesting word histories such as how both *crochet* and *croquet* derive from the word for *hook* (*crook*).

-*ette*	-*et silent*	-*et sounded*
brunette	**ballet**	**banquet**
cassette	beret	bracelet
barrette	bouquet	faucet
omelette	buffet	goblet
vignette	chalet	prophet
cigarette	croquet	velvet
silhouette	gourmet	sonnet
	crochet	couplet
	sachet	

Extend

You may want to share a little history of the English language and explain that for several hundred years French was the official language of England. We should not be surprised that we have many words that are French in origin, especially words having to do with food (*buffet, fillet, gourmet*) and fashion (*beret, brunette, barrette*). The -*ette* ending has been attached to other words to suggest a small or feminine form of something: *dinette, diskette, kitchenette, roomette, novelette, suffragette, majorette* (compare to *drum major*).

Students can be asked to illustrate many of these words and they may want to look for images online. It is easier to understand what a *chalet* is by seeing a picture than it is by reading the definition.

Additional Words. *baguette, coquette, croquette, etiquette, gazette, layette, marionette, quartette, rosette, toilette, vinaigrette, bidet, cachet, fillet, parquet, ricochet, valet, amulet, baronet, cadet, coronet, couplet, eaglet, gauntlet, minaret, scarlet, turret*

ASSESSMENT 8 FOR SORTS 50–55

Ask students to spell and define the following words.

1. confident
2. hesitancy
3. replaceable
4. obedience
5. laughable
6. canceled
7. feasible
8. assistant
9. gourmet
10. fragrance
11. cassette
12. undeniable
13. emergency
14. reversible
15. preferred

SORT 50   Suffixes (*-ent/-ence, -ant/-ance*)

-ent	*-ence*	*-ant*	*-ance*
absent	**absence**	**fragrant**	
fragrance	confidence	patient	
assistant	distance	dominance	
patience	intelligence	confident	
different	prominent	assistance	
distant	difference	defiance	
dominant	prominence	obedient	
intelligent	obedience	defiant	

SORT 51   Suffixes (-*ent*/-*ence*/-*ency*, -*ant*/-*ance*/-*ancy*)

-*ent*/-*ence*/-*ency*		-*ant*/-*ance*/-*ancy*
resident	residence	residency
abundant	abundance	brilliance
competent	emergency	lenient
brilliant	hesitance	competence
emergent	brilliancy	leniency
lenience	competency	abundancy
hesitant	hesitancy	emergence

SORT 52   Suffixes (-able, -ible)

-able	*-ible*	*oddball*
enjoyable	**invincible**	**formidable**
predictable	profitable	edible
perishable	punishable	adaptable
eligible	questionable	laughable
terrible	plausible	attainable
indelible	corruptible	feasible
compatible	decipherable	intangible
sustainable	combustible	reproducible

SORT 52   Suffixes (-able, -ible)

SORT 53   Adding -able and -ible (e-Drop and y to i)

drop e	keep e	y to i	e-drop + -ible
reusable	noticeable		reliable
sensible	unimaginable		adorable
enforceable	knowledgeable		undeniable
defensible	exchangeable		replaceable
excusable	undesirable		identifiable
agreeable	manageable		salvageable
variable	pleasurable		reversible
consumable	responsible		valuable

SORT 54   Accent and Doubling

double		do not double
omitted	**orbited**	benefiting
leveled	propellant	preferred
modeling	concurring	conference
forgetting	beginner	referred
deference	compelling	editing
piloting	forbidden	deferred
reference	repellant	canceled
conferred	preference	limited

Sort 55   Words from French

-ette	*-et sounded*	*-et silent*
brunette	**banquet**	**ballet**
bracelet	cassette	faucet
beret	gourmet	barrette
goblet	bouquet	croquet
chalet	omelette	prophet
vignette	velvet	cigarette
crochet	sonnet	buffet
couplet	silhouette	sachet

Unit IX   Prefix Assimilation

NOTES FOR THE TEACHER

Background and Objectives

The final sorts address assimilated or "absorbed" prefixes. An excellent illustration of a teacher guiding students to an understanding of this phenomenon may be found in Chapter 8 of *WTW* and on the *WTW* video. Prefix assimilation accounts for many spelling errors made by advanced spellers in words such as *accommodation* or *supplement* where the double letters at the beginning of the word often pose problems. Most adults are unaware of this spelling feature even though it occurs in hundreds of words. Understanding how to spot and interpret these "disguised" prefixes will enable students to not only spell the words correctly but to unpack their meaning as well. Students will:

- Identify and spell assimilated prefixes
- Demonstrate an understanding of the meaning of prefixes and words covered in these sorts

Targeted Learners

These sorts are designed for students in the late derivational relations stage who are typically in middle school and high school and have considerable background knowledge about spelling, meaning, connections, roots, and affixes. The assessment on page 148 can be used as a pretest as well as a posttest.

Teaching Tips

Make word hunts in reading materials ongoing so that students continue to add to them over time. Students can easily search for these assimilated prefixes in a dictionary but should look for those whose meaning they understand.

Throughout this unit review roots and affixes. Ask students to use a dictionary or other source of etymological information to investigate word origins. Add new roots to your chart as they are discovered.

The games Assimilie and Rolling Prefixes described in Chapter 8 of *WTW* are designed to review this feature.

SORT 56   PREFIX ASSIMILATION (*IN-*)

Sort and Reflect

(See page 149.) Before sorting discuss the meaning of a few of the words: *incorrect* means "not correct," *immobile* means "not mobile," and so forth. Remind students how they have known about the meaning and function of the prefix *in-* for quite a long time. Now the students will explore why the spelling of the prefix *in-* changes, even though the prefix keeps the same meaning.

Ask students to sort by the first two letters of the word. After sorting ask the students to look at the words in the *im-*, *il-*, and *ir-* columns. Do they see any clues as to why the spelling changes? Students usually notice the spelling of the first letter in the base words. In the *in-* column, however, why *doesn't* the spelling change? Have the students discuss this for a few moments. Occasionally a student *will* in fact come up with the explanation; if they remain stumped, however, then proceed as follows. (See also the teacher explanation in Chapter 8 of *WTW*.) Ask the students to try pronouncing several of the words in the *im-*, *il-*, and *ir-* columns *without* the spelling change in *in-*: *inmobile, inpatience, inlegal, inregular*. Discuss how that feels odd or awkward—the tongue has to make a rapid change from the /n/ sound to the sound at the beginning of each word. Tell the students that this same awkwardness in pronunciation occurred in Latin over 2,000 years ago; so over time, the sound of /n/ became assimilated or "absorbed" into the sound at the beginning of the word to which *in-* was attached, and eventually the spelling changed to reflect this assimilation. In most words in the *in-* column, the pronunciation is not as awkward. A student may note that *incorrect* is a bit hard to say: Why isn't it *iccorrect*? Someday it may be— though you may wish to point out that the spelling system has changed far less since the printing press was invented, because the printed standard has tended to conserve existing spellings and spelling patterns.

in-	*im-*	*il-*	*ir-*
incorrect	**immobile**	**illegal**	**irresistible**
inactive	immoral	illicit	irremovable
inaccurate	immature	illogical	irrational
incapable	immediate	illegitimate	irresponsible
innumerable	imperfect		irreplaceable
insecure	impartial		irregular
indecent	impatient		

Extend

Several of these words include *-able/-ible*. You may wish to review these suffixes with these words.

Additional Words. *inappropriate, incompetent, inescapable, inefficient, immaterial, immodest, immovable, immeasurable, immerse, immense, imminent, immune, immigrant, immoderate, immortal, impaired, impart, impasse, impediment, impersonal, impossible, impractical, improbable, improper, illuminate, illustrious, irreconcilable, irreparable, irreligious, irreducible, irrefutable, irrigation*

SORT 57   PREFIX ASSIMILATION (*COM-*)

Background Information

(See page 150.) Recall that *com* means "with" or "together." The same historical process applies to these words as to the words in the previous sort. Students continue to develop their understanding of this process when they try to pronounce, for example, the following: *comllide* or *comrelate*. *Com-* comes before roots or base words that start with *m* or other bilabial sounds such as *p* or *b*. *Com-* changes to *col-* before *l*, and to *cor-* before *r*. These words pose spelling challenges to students because of the double letters. *Com-* changes to *co-* before vowels and *h* and changes to *con-* before a variety of other consonants. Except for *connection* these usually pose little spelling problem for students because there is no silent letter.

Sort and Reflect

Students should be able to sort these easily after being introduced to assimilated prefixes in the last sort. The *co-* form might give them a little trouble but they will understand the meaning of *coexist* or *coauthor*. Review the prefix *com-* and its meaning. Then talk about the meaning of specific words they know and speculate about others. Select some words to look up for the meaning and derivation. Recall that *mit* means "send" so to form a *committee* "sends the members together" while *convention* means "come together."

com-	col-	cor-	co-	con-
commune	**collaborate**	**correlate**	**coexist**	**confer**
committee	collide	correspond	coauthor	convention
combination	collapse	corrupted	cohesive	connection
commotion	collage	corrosive	coordinate	confide
commitment			cohort	
complement			coincidence	

Extend

Contrast the often confused homophones *complement* and *compliment*. Challenge students to come up with a mnemonic strategy for remembering their meanings.

Ask students to use a dictionary or other source of etymological information to look for both familiar roots (such as *mot* in *commotion*) and new roots (such as *fid* in *confident* which means "trust," as in *fidelity*).

Additional Words. companion, combustion, complementary, component, composite, compensate, commerce, collate, collateral, collection, college, colleague, collision, collusion, corroborate, corrugated, correspondent, correction, corrigible, coagulate, coalition, co-education, coerce, cohabit, coherent, coincide, coordinate, conductor, conflict, confident, confidence, confound, conjugal, conjunction, conscience, conscious, consonant, conspire, consort, constellation, construction, contain, converge, convergent, convenient

SORT 58   PREFIX ASSIMILATION (*SUB-*)

(See page 151.) The prefix *sub-*, introduced in Sort 4, means "under" or "below." It predictably changes to *suf-*, *sup-*, and *suc-* before a root that begins with *f*, *p*, or *c*. These pose the most challenge for the speller. *Sub-* also changes to *sus-* before a variety of consonants but does not form any doubled letters.

Sort and Reflect

Sort and discuss this sort in a manner similar to the previous sorts.

sub-	suf-	sup-	suc-	sus-
subversive	**suffix**	**support**	**succumb**	**suspect**
subjugate	suffer	suppress	successive	sustain
subdue	suffrage	supplement	succinct	suspense
subconscious	suffocate	supplant		susceptible
suburban		supplies		
subsidize				
subcommittee				
submissive				

Additional Words. *substitute, subtraction, subconscious, subculture, subdivide, subjection, subordinate, subsequent, subservient, subsidy, substandard, substructure, subterranean, subversion, sufferable, sufferance, suffice, suffuse, supply, supplicant, supplementary, supportive, suppository, suppression, surreptitious, success, succeed, succession, successful, succor, suspension, suspicion, suspicious, sustenance, suspender*

SORT 59   PREFIX ASSIMILATION (*EX-*, *OB-*)

(See page 152.) The prefix *ex-* means "out," "out of," or "beyond." It poses a spelling challenge when it changes to *ef-* before *f*. The prefix *ob-* means "against" or "in the way" and this meaning is clear in words like *obstruction* or *objection*. Here we look at words where *ob-* changes to *op* before *p*, *of* before *f*, and *oc* before *c*. *Ex* can also change to *ec-* as in *eccentric*, and the *x* is dropped in *eject*, *emotion*, and *erode*.

Sort and Reflect

Sort and discuss in a manner similar to the previous sorts. *Ob-* is a prefix that has not been studied previously, but words like *obstruct*, *objection*, and *opposite* offer good clues to its meaning. *Opportunity* is a curious word with the root *port* meaning "carry to." It has a more positive connotation than most of the *ob-* words. Add *ob-* to your prefix chart.

ex-	ef-	ob-	op-	of-	oc-
expenditure	**effusive**	**obstruction**	**opponent**	**offend**	**occupy**
exaggerate	effort	obsolete	opposite	offensive	occurred
excessive	effervescence	objection	opportunity		occasion
excavate	efficient	obnoxious			
excursion		obstinate			
excrete					
extraction					

Extend

Review why the *r* is doubled before the *ed* in *occurred*. In this word we see two doubling principles at work.

Additional Words. *exit, extract, exceed, exception, excerpt, exclaim, exclamation, exclude, exhume, exile, expand, expansion, expenditure, extend, extinct, extension, exclusion, efface, efferent, effrontery, effigy, effluent, object, objectionable, obligation, obscure, observation, obtain, obvious, opposition, oppression, oppressive, offer, offense, officious, occasionally, occupation, occurrence, occult*

SORT 60   PREFIX ASSIMILATION (AD-)

(See page 153.) The prefix *ad-* is one of the most common prefixes in our language but it is often obscured by assimilation and takes many forms. Any double letters after an initial *a* are a good sign that the prefix *ad-* is hidden there. *Ad-* also takes on different shades of meaning but generally suggests "to" or "toward" as in *advertise* which means literally "turn to." In this sort the assimilated forms *ap-*, *as-*, *at-*, and *ac-* are covered. Others include *af-* (*affix*), *ag-* (*aggression*), *al-* (*allocate*), *an-* (*annex*), and *ar-* (*arrest*).

Sort and Reflect

Students can readily sort these words by the beginning letters. The prefix *ad-* has not been covered specifically in previous sorts so ask students to read through the words to get a sense of what it might mean. Discuss word meanings and select some words to look up in the dictionary to confirm the meanings of the words and the prefix.

You may wish to tell the students that *accommodate* is one of the words most frequently misspelled by highly literate adults: They usually leave out one *m* or *c*. Walking through its etymology *may* help this confusion; at the very least, it will provide students with more information to associate with the spelling. *Accommodate* contains two prefixes (*ac-* and *com-*) added to the root *mod*, which accounts for the double letters (*cc* and *mm*). *Accommodate* is related to *commodious* (literally, "to measure with"), which means "spacious, roomy," and so *accommodate* has come to mean "to make room for." When you *accommodate* someone you "make room for" them or for their wishes, ideas, or point of view.

ad-	ap-	as-	at-	ac-
advertise	**approach**	**associate**	**attentive**	**accompany**
administer	approximate	assignment	attract	accommodate
advice	appoint	assertive	attribute	accelerate
addictive	appendage		attempt	accumulate
adhesive	apprentice			
additional	appreciate			
adjoining				

Extend

Pull out the words ending in *-ate* (*appreciate, accumulate, associate, accelerate*) and identify those that can be both a verb and an adjective depending upon how the suffix is pronounced.

Word hunts will be very productive. Students should be encouraged to investigate any word that begins with an *a* followed by double consonants and to add to the assimilated forms covered in this sort.

Students should now be ready to play the game Assimilie, modeled after Monopoly and described in Chapter 8 of *WTW*.

Additional Words.   *admire, address, adjacent, admit, admission, advise, addict, adjudicate, adjustment, advocate, apparent, appear, applaud, appropriate, approve, appeal, appendix, appreciation, approximation, assail, assault, assemble, assent, assert, assign, assimilate, assist, association, assessment, asset, assurance, attack, attain, attend, attention, attendance, attest, attire, attraction, attractive, attest, attribute, attrition, attuned, access, acceptable, accident, accomplish, account, accustomed, acquisition, acquire*

ASSESSMENT 9 FOR SORTS 56–60

Ask students to spell and define the following words.

1. immediate	2. complement	3. excessive
4. correspond	5. irregular	6. opponent
7. attraction	8. suspense	9. efficient
10. suffocate	11. coordinate	12. accommodate
13. occasion	14. adhesive	15. incorrect

SORT 56   Prefix Assimilation (*in-*)

in-	*im-*	*il-*	*ir-*

incorrect	**immobile**	**illegal**
irresistible	immoral	inactive
inaccurate	immediate	impatient
immature	irremovable	incapable
illicit	innumerable	illogical
indecent	irresponsible	insecure
imperfect	illegitimate	impartial
irrational	irreplaceable	irregular

SORT 57   Prefix Assimilation (*com-*)

com-	*col-*	*cor-*	*co-*	*con-*

commune	**collaborate**	**correlate**
coexist	**confer**	committee
collide	correspond	collapse
coauthor	combination	coordinate
commotion	coincidence	complement
collage	convention	corrupted
cohesive	commitment	confide
corrosive	connection	cohort

SORT 58   Prefix Assimilation (*sub-*)

sub-	*suf-*	*sup-*	*suc-*	*sus-*

sub-		sup-		sus-
subversive		**support**		**suffix**
succumb		**suspect**		subjugate
suffer		supplement		suppress
sustain		successive		subdue
suspense		subconscious		suffrage
suffocate		susceptible		supplant
succinct		subcommittee		suburban
submissive		subsidize		supplies

SORT 59   Prefix Assimilation (*ex-*, *ob-*)

ex-	ef-	ob-	op-	of-	oc-
effusive		**expenditure**		**opponent**	
offend		**obstruction**		**occupy**	
obsolete		exaggerate		effort	
offensive		occurred		objection	
excavate		effervescence		opposite	
obnoxious		opportunity		excursion	
excrete		occasion		efficient	
excessive		extraction		obstinate	

SORT 60   Prefix Assimilation (*ad-*)

ad-	ap-	as-	at-	ac-
advertise	**approach**	**associate**		
attentive	**accompany**	administer		
advice	approximate	assertive		
attribute	accumulate	addictive		
appoint	assignment	accelerate		
adhesive	appendage	attempt		
apprentice	accommodate	adjoining		
additional	attract	appreciate		

Appendix

Blank Sort Template

Independent Word Study

Word Sort Corpus

Blank Sort Template

Independent Word Study

Name _____ Date _____

Cut apart your words and sort them first. Then write your words below under a key word.

_____

_____

_____

_____

_____

_____

_____

_____

_____

What did you learn about words from this sort?

_____

_____

_____

On the back of this paper write the same key words you used above. Ask someone to shuffle your word cards and call them aloud as you write them into categories. Look at each word as soon as you write it. Correct it if needed.

Check off what you did and ask a parent to sign below.
_____ Sort the words again in the same categories you did in school.
_____ Write the words in categories as you copy the words.
_____ Write the words into categories as someone calls them aloud.
_____ Find more words in your reading that have the same sound and/or pattern. Add them to the categories on the back.
                    Signature of Parent _____

Word Sort Corpus: Numbers refers to the sort in which the word appears

1419 words

Word	Sort	Word	Sort	Word	Sort	Word	Sort
abduct	35	amphibious	40	auditory	31	burial	11
abrupt	32	amusement	8	Australian	7	calligraphy	28
absence	50	analyze	13	autobiography	40	canceled	54
absent	50	announce	49	autograph	28	capital	38
absorbency	51	announcement	49	avenue	41	capitalization	38
abstain	49	ante meridian	36	ballet	60	capitalize	13
abstention	49	antebellum	36	banquet	60	capitol	38
abundance	51	antedate	36	barometer	29	captain	38
abundancy	51	anterior	36	barrette	60	cassette	60
abundant	51	antibiotic	40	beautification	17	casual	10
accelerate	59	antipathy	44	beautiful	12	casualty	10
accidental	11	apathy	44	beautify	13	category	9
acclaim	23	apologize	13	beginner	54	cave	19
acclamation	23	appendage	59	believable	53	cavity	19
accommodate	59	application	17	believer	7	centennial	26
accompany	59	appoint	59	benediction	36	centigrade	26
accumulate	59	appreciate	59	benefactor	36	centimeter	26
active	10	apprentice	59	beneficial	36	centipede	38
activity	10	approach	59	benefit	36	century	9
adaptable	52	approximate	59	benefiting	54	century	26
addictive	59	arrival	11	benevolent	36	certain	10
addition	17	artifact	34	beret	60	certainty	10
additional	59	artist	7	betrayal	11	chalet	60
adhesive	59	Asian	7	biblical	42	cheerful	12
adjoining	59	aspect	30	bibliography	42	choreography	28
adjudicate	42	aspiration	41	bibliophile	42	cigarette	60
adjunct	41	assertive	59	bicentennial	26	circumference	45
administer	59	assignment	59	biceps	25	circumnavigate	45
admiration	20	assistance	50	biennial	25	circumscribe	45
admire	20	assistant	50	bifocals	25	circumspect	45
admirer	7	associate	59	bilingual	25	circumstance	45
admit	33	assume	23	bimonthly	25	circumvent	45
adopt	15	assumption	23	binary	25	civilian	7
adoption	15	asterisk	39	biodegradable	40	civilize	13
adorable	53	asteroid	39	biography	40	classify	13
advertise	59	astrology	39	biology	40	cleaner	6
advice	59	astronaut	39	biome	40	cleanest	6
advocate	43	astronomy	39	biotic	40	clinic	15
aerial	39	athlete	19	bisect	25	clinician	15
aerobatics	39	athletic	19	blindness	8	coastal	11
aerobics	39	attacker	7	bomb	18	coauthor	56
aeronaut	39	attain	49	bombard	18	coexist	56
aerosol	39	attainable	52	bouquet	60	cohesive	56
aerospace	39	attempt	59	bracelet	60	cohort	56
affluence	35	attend	49	bravely	5	coincidence	56
afternoon	2	attention	49	bravery	9	collaborate	56
aftertaste	2	attentive	59	breath	19	collage	56
afterthought	2	attract	32	breathe	19	collapse	56
afterword	2	attraction	59	breathless	8	collect	14
aggressive	32	attribute	59	brilliance	51	collection	14
agreeable	53	audible	31	brilliancy	51	collide	56
agreement	8	audience	31	brilliant	51	column	18
allegiance	42	audiotape	31	brunette	60	columnist	18
alliterative	48	audiovisual	31	brutal	21	combination	56
alphabetic	11	audition	31	brutality	21	combine	4
		auditorium	31	buffet	60	combustible	52

comical	11	consumption	23	deferred	54	disorder	1
commemorate	43	container	49	defiance	50	dispirited	41
commitment	56	contradict	31	defiant	50	disposable	47
committed	54	convene	41	define	20	disrespect	1
committee	56	convention	41	definition	20	disrupt	32
commotion	56	conversation	35	deflate	3	dissect	41
commune	56	convert	35	deflect	33	dissent	44
companion	4	coordinate	56	deformed	30	distance	50
company	4	corporal	38	defrost	3	distant	50
compatible	52	corporation	38	dehydrated	39	distended	48
compelling	54	corps	38	delegate	42	distort	15
compete	20	corpse	38	delete	3	distortion	15
competence	51	corpulent	38	delightful	12	distract	32
competency	51	correlate	56	delivery	9	diversify	13
competent	51	correspond	56	democracy	22	divide	16
competition	20	corrosive	56	democratic	22	divine	20
complement	56	corrupted	56	demote	32	divinity	20
compose	20	corruptible	52	denounce	49	division	16
composite	47	couplet	60	dentist	38	dizzily	5
composition	20	create	16	dentures	38	dizziness	8
compound	4	creation	16	denunciation	49	dominance	50
comprehend	16	creator	7	depend	46	dominant	50
comprehension	16	credence	34	deposit	47	dormitory	9
compress	4	credible	34	depression	46	eagerly	5
compression	45	crime	19	deprive	3	earlier	6
comrade	4	criminal	19	desert	15	earliest	6
conceive	49	critic	24	desertion	15	ecology	29
conception	49	critical	24	design	18	edible	52
conclude	16	criticize	24	designate	18	edict	31
conclusion	16	crochet	60	desolate	44	editing	54
concurring	54	croquet	60	detain	49	edition	17
conductor	35	crumb	18	detention	49	editorial	11
confer	56	crumble	18	detract	32	educate	35
conference	54	crummier	6	diameter	29	effervescence	58
conferred	54	crummiest	6	dictate	31	efficient	58
confess	14	custodian	20	dictator	31	effort	58
confession	14	custody	20	dictionary	31	effusive	58
confide	56	dampen	13	difference	50	egress	32
confidence	50	dangerous	12	different	50	eject	33
confident	50	decade	26	diffuse	46	electric	15
conform	30	decapitate	38	digest	15	electrician	15
confuse	46	decathlon	26	digestion	15	eligible	52
conjunction	41	deceive	49	digress	32	emergence	51
connect	14	deception	49	diminish	37	emergency	51
connection	56	decide	22	director	7	emergent	51
consecutive	35	decimal	26	directory	9	emissions	33
consequence	35	decimate	26	disaster	39	emoticon	32
consideration	17	decipherable	52	disbelief	1	emotion	32
consistent	47	decision	22	disconnect	1	empathy	44
conspiracy	20	decorate	16	discourage	1	emphasis	22
conspiracy	41	decoration	16	discredit	34	emphatic	22
conspire	20	decorator	7	discuss	14	employment	8
constitution	47	decrease	3	discussion	14	emptier	6
construct	14	deduct	35	disease	1	emptiest	6
construction	14	defender	7	dishonest	1	emptiness	8
consumable	53	defensible	53	dislocate	47	enable	4
consume	23	deference	54	dismal	36	encourage	4

Appendix

endanger	4	extract	32	general	21	hypersensitive	27
energize	13	extraction	58	generality	21	hyperventilate	27
enforce	4	extraterrestrial	39	generate	40	identifiable	53
enforceable	53	extravert	35	generation	40	identification	17
enjoyable	52	facilitate	34	generic	40	idolize	13
enlarge	4	facsimile	34	generously	5	ignite	19
entrust	4	factory	34	genesis	40	ignition	19
envious	12	falsely	5	genetic	40	illegal	55
equanimity	37	falsify	13	genre	40	illegible	42
equation	37	familiar	24	geode	29	illegitimate	55
equator	37	familiarity	24	geography	29	illicit	55
equilateral	37	family	24	geometry	29	illiterate	48
equitable	37	famous	12	geothermal	29	illogical	55
equivalent	37	fancier	6	global	11	illustrate	16
erode	16	fanciest	6	glorious	12	illustration	16
erosion	16	fatal	21	goblet	60	imaginable	53
erupt	32	fatality	21	government	8	imaginary	9
espresso	46	faucet	60	graphic	28	imagination	17
establish	47	fearlessness	8	graphite	28	imitate	16
etymology	29	feasible	52	gratification	17	imitation	16
exaggerate	58	February	9	greedily	5	immature	55
examination	17	fertile	21	grocery	9	immediate	55
excavate	58	fertility	21	guardian	7	immemorial	43
exceed	48	festive	10	habit	22	immobile	55
excel	22	festivity	10	habitat	22	immoral	55
excellent	22	fictional	11	harmonize	13	immortal	40
except	24	finalist	7	harsher	6	impartial	55
exception	24	flawless	8	harshest	6	impatient	55
exceptional	24	flexible	33	haste	18	impede	38
excess	3	fluctuate	35	hasten	18	impending	45
excessive	58	fluent	35	headphone	28	imperfect	55
exchangeable	53	fluently	5	heroic	11	import	30
exclaim	23	fluid	35	hesitance	51	important	30
exclamation	23	forbidden	54	hesitancy	51	impress	14
excrete	58	forbidden	13	hesitant	51	impression	14
excursion	58	forefathers	2	historian	7	impressive	46
excusable	53	foreman	2	history	9	impure	46
exhale	3	foresight	2	homophone	28	inaccurate	55
exhaust	3	foretell	2	hopelessness	8	inactive	55
exile	3	forethought	2	horoscope	29	incapable	55
expand	16	foreword	2	hostile	21	incorrect	55
expansion	16	forgetting	54	hostility	21	incredible	34
expectation	17	formal	21	humane	19	incredulous	34
expenditure	58	formality	21	humanity	19	indecent	55
expire	41	format	30	humid	10	indelible	52
explain	23	formation	30	humidity	10	indent	38
explanation	23	formidable	52	humorous	12	individual	21
explode	16	fraction	33	hydrant	39	individuality	21
explore	3	fractious	33	hydrate	39	induce	35
explosion	16	fracture	33	hydraulic	39	industrial	11
export	30	fragrance	50	hydrofoil	39	inexpensive	1
express	14	fragrant	50	hydrogen	39	inflate	3
expression	14	friendliness	8	hymn	18	inflexible	33
expurge	46	frighten	13	hymnal	18	influx	35
extend	48	fruitless	8	hyperactive	27	informal	1
extension	48	furious	12	hyperbole	27	information	17
exterior	3	gene	40	hypercritical	27	infraction	33

infrequent	1	invisible	31	magnetic	11	minimum	37
infusion	46	invitation	20	magnification	37	miniscule	37
inhabit	3	invite	20	magnificent	37	minnow	37
inhale	3	invoke	43	magnitude	37	minor	10
inhuman	1	irrational	55	maladroit	36	minority	10
injection	33	irregular	55	malaria	36	minute	37
inmate	3	irremovable	55	malcontent	36	mischief	1
innumerable	55	irreplaceable	55	malefactor	36	mlsfortune	1
insane	1	irresistible	55	malevolent	36	misjudge	42
inscribe	34	irresponsible	55	malfunction	36	misleading	1
inscription	34	Islamic	11	malice	36	mission	33
insect	41	isolate	44	malicious	36	misspell	1
insecure	55	January	9	manageable	53	mistake	1
insert	15	judgment	42	mandate	22	mistaken	13
insertion	15	judiciary	42	mandate	34	mobile	21
insincere	1	junction	41	mandatory	22	mobility	21
insistent	47	juncture	41	maneuver	34	modality	42
inspection	30	justification	17	manicure	34	mode	42
inspector	30	kilometer	29	manual	34	modeling	54
inspiration	22	kinder	6	manufacture	34	moderate	42
inspiration	41	kindest	6	manure	34	modern	42
inspire	22	knowledgeable	53	manuscript	34	modification	42
instability	47	language	43	marvelous	12	moist	18
install	3	laudable	31	medevac	44	moisten	18
institution	47	laughable	52	medic	44	monolingual	25
intangible	52	lavatory	9	medicine	44	monologue	25
intelligence	50	laziness	8	megadose	27	monopoly	25
intelligent	50	legacy	42	megahit	27	monorail	25
interact	45	legalistic	42	megalopolis	27	monotone	25
intercept	45	legally	42	megaphone	27	monotonous	25
interchange	45	legend	42	memento	43	mortal	40
interior	3	legible	42	memorandum	43	mortgage	40
intermural	45	legislate	42	memorial	11	mortician	40
international	45	lengthen	13	memorial	43	mortified	40
internet	45	lenience	51	memorization	17	motion	32
interpersonal	45	leniency	51	memorize	13	motivate	32
interrupt	32	lenient	51	memory	43	mountainous	12
intersection	41	leveled	54	mental	21	multilingual	43
interstate	45	librarian	7	mentality	21	murkier	6
intervene	41	library	9	merrily	5	murkiest	6
intervention	41	limited	54	metal	22	muscle	18
intramural	45	lingo	43	metallic	22	muscular	18
intrapersonal	45	linguini	43	microbe	27	music	15
intrastate	45	linguist	43	microbiology	40	musical	11
intravenous	45	literal	48	microbus	27	musician	15
introduce	45	literate	48	microcosm	27	mystery	9
introduction	35	literature	48	microfilm	27	mythology	29
introspection	45	local	21	microphone	28	narrate	22
introvert	45	locality	21	microscope	29	narrative	22
invade	16	locate	47	microscopic	27	nation	24
invasion	16	location	47	microsurgery	27	national	24
invent	15	locomotion	47	microwave	27	nationality	24
invention	15	locomotive	32	military	9	natural	19
inventor	7	logical	11	millimeter	29	nature	19
inventory	9	machinery	9	mince	37	necessary	9
invert	35	magic	15	mine	19	nervous	12
invincible	52	magician	15	mineral	19	noticeable	53

notification	17	pendulum	46	precede	2, 48	provoke	43
novel	10	pentagon	26	precise	19	psyche	43
novelty	10	percentage	26	precision	19	psyched	43
obedience	50	perimeter	29	preconceive	49	psychiatrist	43
obedient	50	periodontal	38	preconception	49	psychology	43
object	33	periscope	29	predict	2	public	24
objection	58	perishable	52	predictable	52	publicity	24
obliterate	48	permit	33	prediction	31	publicize	24
obnoxious	58	perpendicular	46	preface	2	punishable	52
obsolete	58	persistent	47	preference	54	punishment	8
obstacle	47	personal	21	preferred	54	purgatory	46
obstinate	58	personality	21	prefix	2	purge	46
obstruction	58	perspective	30	prehistoric	2	purification	17
occasion	58	perspire	41	prejudice	42	purification	46
occupy	58	phonics	28	prepare	2	purify	13
occurred	58	phonograph	28	preposition	2	Puritan	46
octagon	26	photocopier	28	prescribe	34	quadrangle	26
octave	26	photogenic	28	prescription	34	quadruped	26
octet	26	photograph	28	preseason	2	quadruple	26
offend	58	photographer	28	presentation	17	quadruplets	26
offensive	58	photosynthesis	28	preside	22	quarter	26
omelette	60	physical	24	president	22	quartet	26
omitted	54	physicist	24	pressure	46	questionable	52
omnipotent	37	physics	24	presume	23	quieter	6
omniscient	37	piloting	54	presumption	23	quietest	6
omnivore	37	plausible	52	prevent	15	quintessence	26
operate	16	pleasurable	53	prevention	15	quintessential	26
operation	16	podiatrist	38	preventive	41	quintet	26
opponent	58	podium	38	prewar	2	quintuplets	26
opportunity	58	poetic	11	priceless	8	quotation	17
oppose	20	poisonous	12	prisoner	7	rapidly	5
opposite	58	politely	5	privilege	42	reaction	3
opposition	20	politeness	8	proceed	48	readily	5
oppress	14	political	24	procession	48	reappear	3
oppression	14	politician	24	profitable	52	rebellious	12
oppressive	46	politics	24	profuse	46	recede	48
orbited	54	polygamy	37	progenitor	40	receive	23
ordinary	9	polyglot	37	progeny	40	reception	23
organization	17	polygon	37	progress	4, 32	recession	48
original	21	polysyllable	37	project	33	reclaim	3, 23
originality	21	polytechnic	37	projector	33	reclamation	23
orthodontist	38	portable	30	prominence	50	reconsider	3
orthopedic	38	portfolio	30	prominent	50	reduce	35
outrageous	12	position	47	promote	4, 32	reference	54
paragraph	28	possess	14	pronounce	49	referred	54
partition	17	possession	14	pronunciation	49	reflect	33
pathetic	44	post meridian	36	propel	4	reflector	33
pathology	44	postbellum	36	propellant	54	reflex	33
patience	50	postdate	2	prophet	60	reform	30
patient	50	posterior	36	proposal	47	regenerate	40
patriotic	11	postmortem	36	propose	4	regress	32
payment	8	postpone	2, 36	prospector	30	reject	33
pedal	38	postscript	36	protect	4, 14	relaxation	17
pedestal	38	postseason	2	protection	14	reliable	53
pedestrian	38	posttest	2	provider	4	relocate	47
pedicure	38	postwar	2	provocation	43	remedial	44
pendant	46	powerlessness	8	provocative	43	remedy	44